The Book of the
COUNTY 4-6-0s

By
Ian Sixsmith

The boiler of 8F 48474 meets its offspring, the 'Standard No.15' boiler of 1014... Colour Rail.

Irwell Press Ltd.

Acknowledgements

This is the second 'Book Of' to describe a Great Western class and it is a cause for rejoicing or lamentation, according to taste, that the detail variation within the class is minimal, at least compared to the devilish Castle brew. The Counties were completed in under two years, remarkably quickly for the Great Western, which rather liked to build its engines over generations. So no 'joggled' frames, fluted cylinder casings or a mysterious voyage through two, three, four row superheater boilers and occasionally back again. But I hope one or two revelations – the much-prized 'nuggets' – have emerged. These would have been misunderstood or overlooked without the help and advice of Mr Brian Penney (still the only man I know who has actually used Zeiss optical gear to align GW main frames) and Mr E.S. Youldon. Also to be heartily thanked are Mr Allan C. Baker and Mr Peter Groom.

Mr Richard Derry of Minehead undertook the daunting task of compiling the tables, for which I cannot thank him enough. It should be arranged for an Engine History Card to be incorporated into his family coat of arms.

The Counties may not be extinct for much longer! 1014 COUNTY OF GLAMORGAN is steadily taking shape – SEE: The County Project, Great Western Society, Didcot Railway Centre, Didcot, Oxfordshire. Tel: +44 (0)1235 817200; drc@didcotrailwaycentre.co.uk

Contents

A County returning to its days of pomp, on the Cornishman about 1960. transporttreasury.co.uk

3

The new locomotive, as portrayed in *The Railway Gazette*. The wartime slightly *ersatz* paper makes for a rather greyer image than we'd have hoped but the clarity is good enough for our annotations to make sense.

CAB

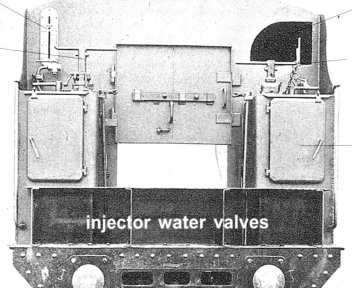

boiler pressure

injector steam valves

drivers brake valve

GWR ATC

sight feed lubricator(cylinders and valves)

TENDER

tender water capacity

water scoop

fire iron tunnel

hand brake

tool/baggage box

injector water valves

water

brake cross beam

Carriage Warming (CWA) pipe

Introduction
'A Noteworthy Departure'

Is how *The Railway Gazette* in August 1945 described the new 4-6-0 1000; it was the forerunner of the 1000 class with, as yet, no mention of 'Counties'. The new locomotive 1000 represented the first new class for which F.W. Hawksworth could take the entire responsibility. The locomotive was a complete surprise to the public, apparently, the design having been worked out and construction embarked upon, 'in secrecy' at Swindon, according to *The Railway Gazette*. All it had to go on, apparently, were 'the many rumours which were in circulation about the new design'. Despite this talk of secrecy *The Railway Observer* seemed well enough aware of what was going on. Back in the summer of 1944 the journal had noted that Lot 354 would be a new series of 6ft 3in 4-6-0 with increased boiler pressure, numbered in the 99XX series. As early as May 1945 it was able to report that 'the new 99XX 4-6-0' was in fact under construction, that the first ten (later increased to 20) were indeed to Lot No.354, that they would have 18½in

No.9900 that might have been. 1000 COUNTY OF MIDDLESEX in black in March 1953, after overhaul at Swindon. The curious swirls on the roof are '1000' in chalk, to make sure the roof sections come together on the right engine upon reassembly. Note sliding roof ventilator, speedometer driven off rear right-hand driving wheel, route/loading classification red D disc (it was briefly originally 'E') and X added later to permit of higher loadings. Prominent is the washout plug cover (one of two – the other is just out of sight) over the feedwater tray, on top of the boiler in front of the safety valve cover. Prominent vacuum pump driven off crosshead. This was a more or less standard GWR feature – most of its engines had them in place of a small ejector. Whistle shield but whistle itself obscured. The two sides of a County presented quite different appearances. Here, on the right-hand side, we have a nameplate mounted separately from the splasher, a reversing shaft, the vacuum ejector pipe, vacuum pump, speedometer and pipe casing above the handrail. The left-hand side was positively plain by comparison. Under the casing bridging the boiler and the smokebox is both the blower pipe, the oil pipes to the cylinders and the Swindon design of smokebox-mounted regulator in the superheater header. The GWR wanted to maintain the clean lines of its engines, so the oil and steam pipes from the cab to the smokebox were hidden within the space between the boiler and its lagging plates; on other railways they were simply run along the boiler for all the world to see. However the GWR's concealed piping had to emerge, to be partly hidden again behind those cover plates, to get from the side of the boiler into the smokebox. Holcroft tells us all about cleaning up the external lines of Great Western engines in his books; in fact Churchward specifically charged him with such a task. GW engines, in most cases, had hydrostatic sight feed displacement lubricators mounted in the cab. They were cab mounted as they had to be controlled by the driver. When the Kings and Castles had their superheat increased, as this required increased oil supply to valves and pistons to prevent scouring of the liners, mechanical lubricators were fitted and these can be observed on photographs. This of course, took matters out of the control of drivers as the amount of the oil feed was predetermined. With the hydrostatic displacement type, not only could the driver adjust the feed, he could also see how much was passing and when the engine was stationary he could shut off the supply; otherwise, unlike a mechanical lubricator driven from the motion, oil would continue to be fed. However, the GWR developed a system whereby the steam feed to the lubricator was controlled by the regulator, so that when it was closed it shut off the steam supply to the lubricator. There was a special regulator position for coasting, so that oil would continue to flow. For whatever reason (cost probably) when the Counties had their superheat increased, the hydrostatic lubricator was retained but it would have been necessary to adjust this so as to feed an increased level of oil for the same reason as with the other classes. It might even have involved a larger lubricator which, in any event, would have been less expensive than fitting mechanical ones. This required additional and/or larger oil pipes, doubtless separate ones MMM for each side of the engine and it was found easier to add an additional 'entry' into the smokebox rather than enlarging the existing one. Hence a second, bottom cover on these engines which will be observed throughout the book – see the next picture/caption for instance.

That no-nonsense front end, on 1006 in the 1960s. Observe there are now two casings on the boiler/smokebox join – see previous caption to 1000. When built the Standard No.15 boiler had 21 superheater tubes in 3 rows. These boilers retained the 21 large tubes when the double chimney was introduced from 1956 and the boiler pressure reduced to 250psi but from about 1957 most boilers had the superheater tubes increased to 28, in 4 rows. Associated with this increased level of superheating is the extra piping (sometimes covered by square casing, sometimes not) as here on 1006 below the handrail. Thirdly, hidden behind the handrail, is the vacuum ejector pipe, the handrail making a bit of a detour around it as it enters the smokebox. The little pipe running down from it is a drain. Close view of vacuum pump driven off crosshead.

by 30in cylinders, an enhanced boiler pressure of 280psi and the same bogie as the Modified Hall. The 'RO' also knew about the copper capped double chimney on the first one only and the new type of tender – it even knew about the continuous splasher.

The new 1000 (when nearly complete in July there was a report that it would in fact be numbered 10000 rather than 9900 – there must have been some surprise when it eventually appeared bearing 1000) looked very much like any other GWR 4-6-0; a cross between a Hall and a Castle but with something indefinably more purposeful about it, perhaps. The starting point had been the Modified Hall as arrived at with 6959 the year before. Indeed the Modified Hall design was regarded as the 'trial effort' for the Counties – or the 1000 class as we should at this point be calling them, for they were not yet named. Nevertheless the principal feature was the new Standard No.15 boiler, identical in major dimensions to the LMS boiler on the 8Fs, which of course had been building at Swindon. This was not appreciated in the first weeks, when 1000's boiler was described as the first major modification to the long-established 'Swindon No.1' boiler for many years. It involved an unexpected foray into high pressure territory, a 'striking new feature' of 280psi pressure. It was easily a record for the Great Western. The number of superheater flues (21) and tube diameter was the same as the Modified Hall, but the superheat surface was reduced from over 300 sq ft to 265 in the new locomotive. No.1000 had many more small tubes, 198 instead of the Modified Hall's 145, though the diameter was reduced, from 2in to 1¾in. The firebox heating surface increased by a little, some 14 sq ft.

Like the Modified Halls the frames were of plate throughout and the cylinders separately cast with a prefabricated steel saddle plate between the front ends of the frames to give support to the smokebox and front end of the boiler. With the framing above the curve of the running plate at the front and the plate-frame bogie (fabricated centre and independent springing) the kinship with the Modified Hall is clear.

The obvious departure was of course the double blastpipe and chimney, though Swindon made it clear this was a trial, to determine its efficacy. A hidden but important feature and another radical departure was a hopper ashpan, to make servicing easier.

Tenders and Toeholds
And that, really, was 1000. The tender was also worthy of note, for it too represented something of departure from previous practice. It was a completely new pattern, 'far less like a traditional Swindon product than is the engine'. It was the first of the flat sided tenders which later became familiar on other 4-6-0s; it was simpler than contemporary tenders and was entirely of welded construction. It held seven tons of coal and 4,000 gallons of water. They were numbered 2935-2954 (re-numbered 100-119 in December/January 1947) and 120 to 129. The engines went into traffic with tenders largely in sequence apart from 1011 with 2947 and 1012 with 2946. The Hawksworth straight sided County tenders were 8ft 6in wide, whereas similar tenders used with Castles and Halls were only 8ft wide and carried 6 tons of coal and 4,000 gallons of water. 'The absence of a name for the new engine' it was remarked, 'will be a matter of regret to the many admirers of Great Western practice, but this is offset to some extent by the excellent transfer of the company's coat of arms which adorns the tender'. Some firemen were less than wholly

impressed, claiming that the Collett tender encouraged the coal to feed forward more readily.

The wider tender wasn't without its drawbacks. The cab width was naturally made to match that of the tender with the result that the narrow but important toehold at the base of the cab on the outside was all but lost on a County. This was supposedly countered by attaching a single step (the GWR for some unknown reason eschewed the use of leading footsteps on tender engines) to one end of the buffer beam. So if a man was standing alongside the buffer beam on the side away from the step and had to gain the front platform with the loco astride a pit, for smokebox cleaning or whatever, a grand tour was necessary, via the cab! As Eric Youldon points out 'when CHANNEL PACKET appeared in 1941 it also had a leading footstep on just one side but before you could say "Spam Can" (or so it seemed) a duplicate footstep was added on the other side.'

1000, nameless, simply entered the fray of post-war traffic, with sheds presumably grateful for what Dr W.A. Tuplin called a 'two cylinder Castle with a boiler pressure to match the Southern Pacifics.' An Old Oak engine for its first few years it made its first visit to Plymouth at the end of October 1945 with the afternoon Paddington-Penzance express. It was deemed worthy of remark that the following day it took out the normally double-headed eleven coach Plymouth-North of England train unaided.

By March 1946 it became known that the engines would be named Counties, after the fashion of a series of 4-4-0s introduced in 1904, 3800-3839. The new 1000 was naturally the first, to be named COUNTY OF MIDDLESEX, just as 3800 had been before it. The tenders, as originally fitted, were numbered in sequence with the locos; indeed,

The New G.W.R. 4-6-0 No. 1,000

There is a peculiar interest in new locomotive designs emanating from Swindon, for it is becoming increasingly clear how much locomotive engineers generally are indebted to many of the ideas which have emanated from that historic railway centre. Mr. Hawksworth's new engine, No. 1000, which is described elsewhere in this issue, has been the subject of many guesses for months past. The official announcement shows it to be not so revolutionary as it was imagined to be in some quarters. The new boiler pressure, 280 lb. per sq. in., brackets it with Mr. Bulleid's 4-6-2s as the most highly pressed in the country. Although the conventional locomotive boiler has been built for higher pressures, this is getting fairly near the limit set by existing materials and methods of construction. The adoption of the double chimney and blast pipe may perhaps be considered as one way in which a railway may repay its debt to another. After Sir William Stanier's elevation to the position of Chief Mechanical Engineer of the L.M.S.R. in 1932, a number of characteristically Great Western features began to appear on the products of Derby and Crewe, where in fact they have become standard practice. Quite recently the double chimney and blast pipe have been applied successfully on the L.M.S.R., particularly to the rebuilt "Royal Scot" class; and now the compliment is returned by the construction of the first Swindon engine with that arrangement. The tender of No. 1000 is of great interest; to have produced a design with a full weight of 49 tons and an empty weight of only 22 tons 14 cwt. is an achievement which reflects great credit on all concerned.

* * * *

engagingly, each tender was erected on the pit adjacent to its particular engine. From the beginning the thirty making up the class were distributed more or less evenly on the GW's principal main lines, going to London, Birkenhead, Bristol and Wales and the West. This seems not the best fashion of distributing them, to modern eyes, though it remained a common way of disposing

steam engines for as long as they were built in this country. The greater saving would have come through concentrating at say, Bath Road and Old Oak; for spares/maintenance certainly but also perhaps to get crews working them regularly and with luck working them more economically. It was said in the earlier years, in particular, that the Counties were not particularly good steamers; they could do the jobs given to them but time was easily lost, especially on express passenger turns if restrictions or slacks were encountered en route. This sounds an entirely natural consequence of crews having charge of the new locos only intermittently. Also – though it is a minor point – aids to servicing such as a hopper ashpan meant scant saving if a shedman labouring on the firepit got one every two or three shifts; half a dozen *every* shift might have made a local difference. As it was, men were expected to deal with a set number of 'big' and/or 'small' locos and that was it.

1017 and 1018 were named almost immediately (some of the earlier ones took until 1948 to get plates) but were nameless while on trials. Fifty-five Halls built nameless had the class painted on the centre splasher until plates were fitted. Likewise the six de-named Stars and it seems curious that the temporarily nameless Counties were not similarly

1021 COUNTY OF MONTGOMERY on shed; red D disc but no 'X' now. The anti-vacuum valve on the steam valve offers a wisp of steam; it dropped off its seat when no steam was flowing and stopped the piston drawing in debris from the smokebox. Substantial big end particularly apparent from this angle.

1021 COUNTY OF MONTGOMERY in early BR days, with BRITISH RAILWAYS in full, in GW style. No speedometer yet.

The descent into grime was swift. 1012 COUNTY OF DENBIGH, named in 1946, is as grimy and scruffy as any Western Region 4-6-0 of 1965. Someone has been having fun – WOT CLEANING might be making a point but otherwise it must have been someone smitten to trace SALOME twice in the layers of dirt. Sadly it's no guide to the date of the picture. The first film came out in 1923 and the better known one, with Rita Hayworth, in 1953, far too early and rather too late for 1012 in GW condition. This is believed to be Temple Meads, so perhaps Wilde's play was on in Bristol. The culprit was so impressed he wrote it twice!

1001 COUNTY OF BUCKS at Swindon. The period would be after the fitting of a double chimney at the end of 1957; presumably at its succeeding overhaul in early 1959. 1001 is presumably awaiting entry, for after the work was complete it would normally be progressed along the great wall of A Shop to the turntable to be joined with a tender. The wheels and motion look strangely clean, but there are no giveaway chalk marks.

'labelled'. From thereon the Counties emerged from works fully named. The abbreviated BUCKS, HANTS and so on came about through the need to avoid tautology. As Irwell Press' favourite curmudgeon, Tony Wright, puts it: *What BR did later with some of their diesel/electric namings over the shires was tautology; needless repetition. The GWR got it right (well, eventually) and so did the LNER. 1011 was in fact in danger of starting life as COUNTY OF CHESHIRE, but this blunder was avoided when someone recalled the obloquy which had resulted from the original County 4-4-0 3814 COUNTY OF CHESHIRE, which had to be rectified. 'Shire' and 'county' are of course words for exactly the same thing. So, COUNTY OF CHESHIRE is the same as saying 'County of Chester's County', or 'Shire of Cheshire'. When I were a lad, I asked a teacher why I saw COUNTY OF CHESTER, COUNTY OF STAFFORD, COUNTY OF SALOP, etc, and he explained why. Cornwall, Devon, Somerset, Middlesex and so on, because they didn't have 'shire' in their names were all right, and the prefix 'County of' was quite correct. Most of the others merely took the county town/city as the suffix to 'County of'. However, Wilts and Hants were just abbreviations, and Salop is the ancient name of Shrewsbury. Thank goodness we had some of the splendid Welsh counties remembered; Carmarthen, Brecknock, Radnor, Montgomery and so on. See also the record for 1010.*

Rough Riding

In the summer of 1946 dismaying reports emerged of rough riding on the new 4-6-0s due, it was deemed, to their 'extremely heavy connecting rods'. 1005, it was noted, had been duly rebalanced and at the end of June 1946 would be put on test trains between Bristol and Paddington. While in shops for this work its COUNTY OF DEVON plates were fixed. This all proved misleading, however and the Great Western was quick to point out that there *were no* rough riding problems with the Counties, and that the connecting rods *were not* unduly heavy. The rebalancing was indeed taking place, but was 'experimental' and 'merely represented one of the many experiments which are usual following the production of a new design.' Nonetheless in 1947 an Old Oak driver could declare to Eric Youldon that he wouldn't drive a County in excess of 70mph because of the rough ride.

Dr Tuplin was almost scornful of the high boiler pressures as employed on the Counties, calling it a 'lark'. (The good doctor also averred that high boiler pressures did more work hitting headlines than pushing pistons!) The Southern reduced its Pacific pressures to 250psi and the Western Region followed suit, beginning in 1956. There were thirty-five high pressure boilers for the class, Nos.9900-9929 (matching the

original, as envisaged, number series of the locos) and five extras, Nos.9950-9954. All had 3-row superheaters and 280lb pressure and were classified OA; after 1956 all had the pressure reduced to 250 pounds and most rebuilt with a 4-row superheater from 1957, reclassified OB. This increased superheating surface from 265 (later 248) sq ft to 320 sq ft.

In a letter to *British Railways Illustrated* in April 1995 Eric Youldon wrote: 'C.J. Allen in *The Railway Magazine* for July/ August 1947 included several remarks to the effect that the Counties well, were not exactly worth writing home about. This got back to Hawksworth; he took umbrage and arranged a series of footplate trips for Allen on the new product so he could see for himself how good it was. CJA could never resist a footplate jaunt and to show his appreciation he wrote, after describing his journey in the November/December issue, "The Counties are in every way a worthy and dependable addition to the succession of GWR classes from Churchward on". In fact a table of the performance of 1028 with nine coaches (301/315 tons) said all that was necessary; 9½ mph at the top of Hemerdon and 15 over Dainton. It is only fair to say that the engines came into their own from the mid-1950s following redraughting and invariably gave a good account of themselves.

Perfect lined black on 1019 COUNTY OF MERIONETH, newly painted with the first emblem and red ground to the nameplate. Note BR 83A Newton Abbot shedplate but retention of GW code NA just behind the bufferbeam. Above the top slidebar is, clearly for once, the rocker arm for the inside valve gear. The locos had gravity sanding, to the front of the leading driver and to the rear of the trailing one. A conventional sandbox and filler was mounted under the cab for the rear sanding. The front sandbox was hidden away behind the slidebars, its filler cap barely visible on the top surface of the running plate. The plate frame bogie, as on the Modified Halls, was prominent. It was a retrograde step, many think, for the de Glehn/Churchward bogie was just about the most successful ever. Its use had largely done away with fractures, a flaw that returned with the plate frame bogie. The new driving wheel size was a surprise too, for a new pattern was required and it was another (extremely expensive) item to stock, all for three inches over the Halls. For a time of scarcity, want and austerity it seems an unusual way to have gone.

The tender of 1006 COUNTY OF CORNWALL, in Swindon roundhouse in the 1960s. Those rear edges were more rounded than you'd think...

Above. One of the newly named engines in service, 1008 COUNTY OF CARDIGAN at Cardiff General on 24 August 1947. Apart from the shaded block style number on the bufferbeam the grime renders it almost unidentifiable, despite it being named only a few weeks before. There is a pretty bad leak from the washout cover over the feedwater tray ahead of the safety valve cover. That would be an early use of the train reporting number brackets.

Left. The County plates were unique; they were straight of course but they also varied from side to side. On the left-hand side they were mounted more or less conventionally on the splasher, as on 1023 at Truro. E. Blakey, transporttreasury.co.uk

Left. Mounted the same way on the right-hand side meant they would have been obscured by the reversing lever, so they had to be brought forward and set on a plate, as on 1005 at Taunton on 8 August 1955. Also clearly visible is the linkage to the leading sandbox. J. Robertson, transporttreasury.co.uk

1012 as yet not named, at Reading shed on 1 June 1946; it would get its plates the following month. Single chimney, GW and coat of arms on tender. H.C. Casserley, courtesy R.M. Casserley.

Speedometers

The Counties were built without speedometers but all were eventually equipped with them, from 1950 to 1954. They were of conventional GWR pattern, driven from the right-hand trailing coupled wheel.

Double Chimneys, Eventually

1000 and its 'experimental' double chimney turned out to be the longest draughting 'experiment' in history. At the beginning of 1954, after nearly a decade, 1000 (fitted with indicator shelter) was noted on short test trains between Swindon and Reading with the dynamometer car. This prompted further tests (doubtless springing from the work of S.O. Ell) with both 1007 (on the Test Plant in October 1953) and 1009 from July to November 1954, which included a stint on the Plant. 1009 was fitted with a riveted fabricated 'tin' double stovepipe of singular ugliness. The idea was presumably that its dimensions could be readily altered, or maybe it was deemed wasteful to have a casting made. Thus fitted, with indicator shelter, 1009 ran tests and was put on the test plant on various occasions from July 1954 to the end of the year, though it presumably worked ordinary trains in the meantime. It had been at Neyland when sent to Swindon and in early 1955 was released to Bath Road instead, still with its 'tin' chimney. It was the results of these trials with 1009, rather than the 'experimental' 1000, that the new draughting proportions were arrived at for the class

but even then progress was slow. The double chimney so characteristic of the Counties did not begin general application for well over a year, until 1956, in a process that itself took some three years. It was not a welcome sight in enthusiast circles and, in a time when we could afford to be fussy about aesthetics, *The Railway Observer* condemned the double chimney for being too short and out of proportion with the other boiler fittings. By the time the process of fitting the Counties was complete, they had barely a year or two of front line service left. Provision of double chimneys was as follows:

1000	3/58
1001	12/57
1002	6/58
1003	11/57
1004	4/57
1005	12/58
1006	12/58
1007	5/57
1008	5/58
1009	9/56
1010	1/57
1011	11/58
1012	9/57
1013	2/58
1014	5/58
1015	11/58
1016	3/57
1017	3/59
1018	1/59
1019	3/59
1020	11/58
1021	10/59
1022	5/56
1023	5/57

1024	7/58
1025	8/59
1026	10/58
1027	9/56
1028	8/58
1029	5/59

Incidentally, the experimental double chimney on 1009 had a small third orifice alongside the two main ones. This was for spent steam from the brake ejector. The main series of double chimneys had the third orifice midway between the two chimneys.

Double Chimney Afterthought, or Second Thoughts...

Years later, unlikely as it may seem, in July 1961 the CM&EE Western Region noted that the WR Board Chairman had never been satisfied with the appearance of the double chimney. Despite the lengthening shadows for steam, there was some discussion as to how they could be improved without impairing the performance of the Counties. The possibility of fitting Castle chimneys was discounted due to a number of reasons not least the difference of more than an inch between blast pipe centres. A new pattern would almost certainly have been heavier than any made so far, the Counties having a deeper petticoat inside the smokebox than any other class. Unsurprisingly, by August 1961 any thought of modification was abandoned – the Counties would start being *withdrawn* in a year or so.

Block lettering on bufferbeam of 1014 at Paddington; it had gone new to Bath Road and like others stayed there until dieselisation work began in 1960 and even then moved only to St Philips Marsh, to continue for a while in the same rosters. The Bath Road Counties were thus the ones most regularly to be found in London; others, once the distribution was altered at the beginning of the 1950s, could be rather scarce 'in town'. www.rail-online.co.uk

Lovely dark green on 1019 COUNTY OF MERIONETH at Swindon on 4 April 1946. It had only just emerged from the nearby works, the first of the class to appear already fitted with nameplates. H.C. Casserley, courtesy R.M. Casserley.

1011 COUNTY OF CHESTER at Bristol Temple Meads on 28 August 1948. This was another of the Bath Road stalwarts, spending the great part of their working lives there. H.C. Casserley, courtesy R.M. Casserley.

Re-assembly of 1015 underway at Swindon in October 1954. This would have been one of the last Counties to be outshopped in black. A.R. Carpenter, transporttreasury.co.uk

A sparkling 1029 newly overhauled at Swindon. This was one of the most familiar sights at Swindon; conveniently positioned, in pristine condition and perfect for the light were the overhauled and repainted locomotives outside the vast A shop. Larger locos were traversed out of the side and stabled on these roads alongside the building. Newly painted and not yet fired (the brick arch might not even be fitted yet) 1029 COUNTY OF WORCESTER after this will be re-united with tender and lit up. Genteel trial runs were made to one of two or three established places not too far away (doubtless with a convenient pub) with the Inspector and Fitter riding in the cab and any adjustments or temporary repairs carried out once there. 1029 would then have a fast run back to the works for the trials gang to rectify any defects noted. It was only then that any loco newly overhauled like 1029 went for a running in period on a local working before return to its home shed. There are some interesting differences compared to the 1945-49 green; cab lining no longer to top of the cabside window and firebox bands are unlined. B. Richardson, transporttreasury.co.uk

Testing times for 1009 COUNTY OF CARMARTHEN 1. A phantom fitter (hopefully with earplugs!) observes the dizzying blur of the rotating drivers and the frenzied connecting rod. Note the 'tin' chimney.

Testing times for 1009 COUNTY OF CARMARTHEN 2. At Swindon on 7 November 1954, fitted up with the indicator shelter for work with the dynamometer car and twenty-coach test trains. From the dimensions of the temporary chimney was derived the new double chimney to be fitted to the class. So it was experience with 1009 rather than 1000 (the intended 'test bed', back in 1945) from which the draughting dimensions were finally obtained. Philip J. Kelley.

Restricted to the main lines to Penzance and Wolverhampton nearly a third of the Counties were at Old Oak Common for the first years. All except one was transferred to Laira at the end of 1950 and London's last one went to Chester a couple of years later as wider routes were opened to them. Thereafter they remained at the periphery as it were, in this way replacing (in part at least) Castles on work north of Wolverhampton, say, or west of Plymouth. Here's how they were distributed at first (more or less – this is the summer of 1950 before Old Oak's were dispersed to 'the periphery'):

1000	Old Oak
1001	Neyland
1002	Bath Road
1003	Old Oak
1004	Penzance
1005	Bath Road
1006	Laira
1007	Bath Road
1008	Old Oak
1009	Neyland
1010	Old Oak
1011	Bath Road
1012	Old Oak
1013	Truro
1014	Bath Road
1015	Old Oak
1016	Stafford Road
1017	Stafford Road
1018	Newton Abbot
1019	Newton Abbot
1020	Neyland
1021	Old Oak
1022	Laira
1023	Laira
1024	Stafford Road
1025	Stafford Road
1026	Old Oak
1027	Westbury
1028	Bath Road
1029	Stafford Road

Chester shed got some for the London jobs after 1003 had spent a month's trial in early 1951. From 1952 they worked the Paddington trains as far as Wolverhampton, displacing Castles. Penzance Counties (originally just one)

were at the apex of the shed's workings, to Plymouth and Newton Abbot, the limits of its orbit. Bath Road similarly used its Counties on the principal trains, and 1028 indeed worked the first of the new two hour expresses to Paddington in 1953. As elsewhere, Castles remained in charge of the best work though of course there was usually a lot more of them. Turn and turn about the Counties seemed the equal of the Castles and by the middle 1950s were to be found at Paddington throughout the day on expresses from Bristol. They proved useful wherever they went, it seems, and appeared to find a useful niche on the non-passenger but extremely important heavy milk trains, from both the West of England and the West of Wales. By spring 1955 the distribution looked rather different from five years before:

1000	Bath Road
1001	Neyland
1002	Penzance
1003	Shrewsbury

16

1004	Swindon
1005	Bath Road
1006	Penzance
1007	Truro
1008	Chester
1009	Bath Road
1010	Laira
1011	Bath Road
1012	Laira
1013	Shrewsbury
1014	Bath Road
1015	Laira
1016	Shrewsbury
1017	Stafford Road
1018	Penzance
1019	Swindon
1020	Neyland
1021	Penzance
1022	Chester
1023	Truro
1024	Chester
1025	Shrewsbury
1026	Chester
1027	Neyland
1028	Bath Road
1029	Neyland

So over five years the 'axis', as it were, of workings altered with over a third of the class disappearing from Wolverhampton and London, migrating instead to the 'edge'. By 1960 only Bristol remained as one of the early centres for the class, with eight at St Philips Marsh on duties that would rapidly decline as Bath Road came fully into use as a diesel depot, 1960-61. There were now seven at Shrewsbury, Chester having passed to the LMR and, reflecting the inexorable move of steam to the second ranks, a half dozen at

Swindon and scattered examples at sheds like St Blazey and Exeter. November 1960:

1000	St Philips Marsh
1001	Neyland
1002	St Blazey
1003	Shrewsbury
1004	Swindon
1005	St Philips Marsh
1006	Laira
1007	Exeter
1008	Penzance
1009	St Philips Marsh
1010	Swindon
1011	St Philips Marsh
1012	Swindon
1013	Shrewsbury
1014	St Philips Marsh
1015	Swindon
1016	Shrewsbury
1017	Shrewsbury
1018	Laira
1019	Swindon
1020	Neyland
1021	Swindon
1022	Shrewsbury
1023	Exeter
1024	St Philips Marsh
1025	Shrewsbury
1026	Shrewsbury
1027	St Philips Marsh
1028	St Philips Marsh
1029	Neyland

Liveries

The emergence of 1000 in 1945 marked the first appearance of the pre-war GWR lined dark green (officially 'middle chrome green') but with the tender carrying GW, the letters placed either side of the company coat of arms in place of the pre-war shirt button. The rest, 1001-1029, came out the same, with one exception; 1000 had lining on the running plate valence and a panel of lining on the cylinders. This was a trifle excessive in the time of post-war belt-tightening and were omitted in the subsequent Counties.

From nationalisation to early 1949 the Counties continued to be repainted lined green, with BRITISH RAILWAYS in full, in small characters to a GW style. Lined black was introduced on Counties in early 1949 initially with tenders blank until the lion-and-wheel transfers were introduced in July that year.

Numberplates were affixed to smokebox doors by mid-1951, 1009 and 1017 carrying the regional 'W' suffix for a short time.

From May 1955 lined BR green made its appearance with the first emblem; the second version was introduced from April 1957 and all thirty were eventually turned out in this garb; often called 'Brunswick green' it is better described as BR dark green. The first was 1010, the result of a decision 'to promote Counties to express passenger livery'.

'Give Us More Halls...'

Much as we enjoy studying the variety of engine types and the variety within them, to the question 'did the Counties live up to expectations?' the answer has to be 'no.' Nothing they did in the first decade, until the interminably delayed re-draughting took place at least, could not have been done by a decent Hall.

1000, by now a Bath Road engine, at Old Oak Common shed on 5 May 1956, after a fitful bout of cleaning. Washout plug cover hanging loose on firebox shoulder. The Counties, like the Modified Halls, had plate frames with separate cylinders and a smokebox saddle casting all bolted together rather than the Churchward single cylinder/saddle block and extra frames at the front. It was a reversal of practice heretofore from (some might deem) a proven, successful arrangement. If so it would be hard to see why the change was made but, then again, if Churchward practice *was* so successful by comparison, then no other companies had chosen to adopt it. R.C. Riley, transporttreasury.co.uk

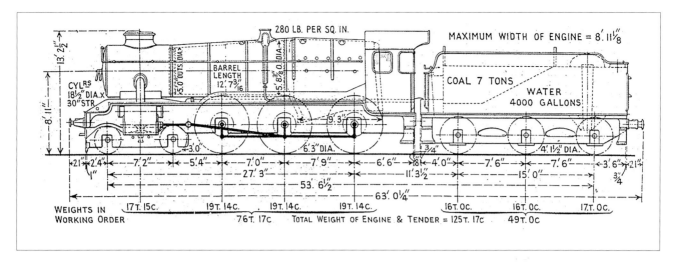

They made no impact locally, certainly in the West of England; they were nameless and, as mentioned, without even COUNTY CLASS stencilled on the splasher and in terms of publicity were put firmly in the shade by the Southern, busily presenting half the towns in the West with their very own bright green Pacifics complete with shields, naming ceremonies and poster campaigns.

From the early publicity one wouldn't have expected to see any more GWR 4-6-0s built – at least in the RED route restriction category and the batches of Counties planned tended to confirm this.
Lot 354 issued for 10 engines 9900-9909 but increased to 20 9900-9919. All built, as 1000-1019.
Lot 358 issued in February 1945 for 15 engines 9920-9934; increased to 30 in June 1945 but reduced to 10 in December 1945 which were built as 1020-1029.
Lot 359 issued for 15 engines but cancelled).
Total planned, 65 engines; total built 30.

So just thirty Counties saw the light of day with the last turned out being 1029 in April 1947 after which things returned to normal (a trifle embarrassingly for Hawksworth) with the ranks of Castles and Halls strengthened by a further 30 and 59 respectively by late 1950. From all this it is hard to avoid the conclusion that the Counties did not much impress their masters. Just what role the County was to play remains obscure. Halls and Castles between them would meet any demand likely to confront the newcomer, though it might have been a different story if the engines had displayed from the start their greatly enhanced performance after the 1957 modifications. We might well have seen all 65, or even more… If all had materialised some further ideas on names would have been necessary as it is unlikely the Western would have been able to come to terms with the likes COUNTY OF KENT or COUNTY DURHAM! Perhaps we would have finally got some cathedrals…

DIMENSIONS 1000	
Cylinders (2) dia.	18½ in.
Cylinders stroke	30in.
Piston valves, dia.	10in.
Wheels, coupled, dia.	6ft 3in.
Wheels, bogie, dia.	3ft 0in.
Wheelbase, coupled	14ft. 9in
Wheelbase, total engine	27ft 3in.
Wheelbase, engine+tender	53ft 6½in.
Boiler dia. max. outside	5ft 8³/₈in.
Boiler dia. min. outside	5ft 0in.
Boiler length of barrel	12ft 7³/₁₆ in.
Boiler working pressure	280lb per sq. in.
Boiler centre line from rail	8ft 11in.
Firebox: inside, top	8ft 7¹⁵/₁₆in x 4ft 9½in.
Firebox: inside bottom	8ft 6in x 3ft 3³/₈in.
Firebox outside, top	9ft 9in x 5ft 10⁷/₈in.
Firebox outside bottom	9ft 3in x 4ft 0in.
Firebox height, front	6ft 8¹¹/₁₆in.
Firebox height, back	5ft 1²³/₃₂in.
Heating surfaces:	
Fire tubes (21 5¹/₈in flues and	
198 1¾ in tubes, 13ft 0in long	1,545 sq. ft
Firebox	169 sq. ft
Total evaporation surface	1,714 sq. ft.
Superheater (84 tubes 1¼ dia.	
12ft 0in long)	265 sq. ft.*
Total combined	1,979 sq. ft.
Grate Area	28.84 sq. ft.
Weight in working order:	
Engine	76 tons 17 cwt.
Tender	49 tons 0 cwt.
Total weight of engine and tender	
In working order	125 tons 17 cwt.
Tractive effort at 85 per cent	
Boiler pressure	32,580lb
Water capacity of tender	4,000 gallons
Coal capacity of tender	7 tons
*3-row; 4-row was 320 sq ft.	

1000 on top-notch work – at Liskeard in May 1957. It carries a 'SC' plate under the shedplate, indicating that it is fitted with BR self cleaning smokebox apparatus. The extent of this fitment in the class (1000 had it at least two years before) and the time it lasted is not clear. M.J. Read, Colour-Rail.

The highest recorded mileage was 794,555 with 1012; average for the class was 672,944 which was respectable enough but not outstanding given their years of service. The GWR faithful never quite took them to heart, although there was some mellowing over time. There were three reasons for this. Firstly that double chimney on 1000 was bit off-putting; secondly lack of beading on the splasher and front edge of the cab gave them a slightly austere look and thirdly the boiler was more LMS than GWR. All in all the 1000s were not the thoroughbreds in the same mould as the other 4-6-0s, or for that matter the panniers.

A Laira engine up in town; 1021 COUNTY OF MONTGOMERY at Old Oak on 24 March 1957. It is a minor curiosity that there was no obvious means of climbing up to the front running plate of a GW 4-6-0 if you wanted to, say, open the smokebox door – witness the 'grand tour' described in the text, and the reasons behind the Counties' little hanging step at the front on one side only, with a single grab iron. The usual way, it turns out, to get to the smokebox end of GWR tender engine was to climb the *cab* steps and walk/edge yourself along the running plate. Front steps on a tender engine were considered an abomination at Swindon. A suitable hand rail was located on the cab side on the Churchward cab and beneath the cab window on the Collett cab. The side framing alongside the cab was about three inches wide, enough to get a good foothold. On the side tank engines the tanks were almost flush with the side framing and access to the front from the cab was not possible; hence tank locos had footsteps at the front end. The County cab was about six inches wider than on a King or Castle which resulted in a very narrow side frame below the cab, too narrow really to get a decent toehold. To discourage staff from taking this hallowed route no side handrail was provided on the Counties and the single front footstep was fitted to give access to the smokebox end. As an aside, while tank engines had conventional steps at the front, they were very difficult to mount; of necessity they were set inwards from the side framing which meant that with your feet on the footstep your knee or shin was hard up against the side framing. To haul yourself up on to the side frame you had to grasp the horizontal hand rail and lever yourself up, often scraping a knee or shin on the thin edge of the plating in the process. Access from the cab end was much easier, and less painful! A.E. Bennett, transporttreasury.co.uk

Two Counties in Swindon roundhouse, 1023 COUNTY OF OXFORD and 1010 COUNTY OF CAERNARVON with 7829 RAMSBURY MANOR in between and a WD to the right, 90355, on 3 June 1962. The class was still intact but withdrawals began at the end of the summer and by the end of the year nigh on a third of the class had gone. The last Counties finished up on sundry duties, like any other WR 4-6-0 and as 1963 got under way their passenger days, at least so far as the higher rated workings were concerned, were over. It took nearly two years for the rest to go, with 1011 standing out as the sole survivor for several months until the end of 1964. www.rail-online.co.uk

1000 COUNTY OF MIDDLESEX with the new, distinctly flared, standard double chimney fitted a few months before. Parcels train, Stapleton Road, 11 October 1958. B.W.L. Brooksbank, Initial Photographics.

The Record

The information herein follows more or less that in the previous 'Book Of' volumes reflecting, largely, what is recorded in the original engine histories, in this case the Swindon Registers at The National Archive. This has been married to the record of *The Railway Observer* and other journals. The codes are as follows:

G General
H Heavy
I Intermediate
L Light
R Thought to be 'Running'

WR/BR equivalents after 1948 were:
HC Heavy Casual
HG Heavy General
HI Heavy Intermediate
LC Light Casual
LI Light Intermediate
U Unclassified
C Casual

Cont 'Continuation' – often called 'Rectification' elsewhere. It is a brief recall to works to attend to some minor (or sometimes not so minor) fault showing up after running in following works attention.

Dates of works/outstation shops visits are those upon which the repairs were deemed complete.

1000 newly emerged at Swindon, in green, 6 November 1955. R. Wilson, transporttreasury.co.uk

1000 COUNTY OF MIDDLESEX with the 10.00am ex-Chester, in the summer of 1951. Black livery, original double chimney. The location is the short cutting between the River Dee bridge (visible through the arches in the background) and Saltney Junction. The train is bound for Shrewsbury and the south. S.D. Wainwright.

1000 COUNTY OF MIDDLESEX

To traffic 4/8/45
Named 3/46

Mileages and Boilers

From new		9900
8/5/47	81,704	9900
14/2/50	193,439	C9913
15/1/52	279,912	C9910
26/3/53	336,835	C9914
10/11/55	423,427	C9908
26/3/58	527,321	C9914
12/2/60	616,076	C9904
14/9/62	691,632	C9914

Sheds and Works

8/9/45	Old Oak
2/10/46	Swindon Works **L**
8/5/47	Swindon Works **L**
25/8/47	Swindon Works **L**
25/9/47	Bath Road Shops **R**
13/10/47	Swindon Works **R**
15/10/48	Swindon Works **L**
27/10/48	Swindon Shed **L**
27/1/49	Old Oak Shops **U**
26/8/49	Swindon Works **U**
4/10/49	Taunton Shops **U**
16/12/49	Old Oak Shops **U**
14/2/50	Swindon Works **HG**
30/3/50	Reading Shops **U**
1/5/50	Old Oak Shops **U**
3/6/50	Bath Road Shops **U**
13/11/50	Old Oak Shops
30/12/50	Laira
11/10/51	Old Oak Shops **U**
15/1/52	Swindon Works **HI**
9/10/52	Laira Shops **U**
1/11/52	Chester
26/3/53	Swindon Works **HG**
27/2/54	Bath Road
22/4/55	Swindon Works **LC**
1/9/55	Swindon Works **U**
10/11/55	Swindon Works **HI**
25/1/57	Swindon Works **HC**
26/3/58	Swindon Works **HG**
27/8/58	Bath Road Shops **U**
12/2/60	Swindon Works **HI**
19/9/60	St. Philips Marsh
4/12/61	Ebbw Jct. Shops **U**
3/2/62	Gloucester Barnwood Shops **U**
25/4/62	St. Philips Marsh Shops **U**
15/9/62	Swindon Works **HG**

Tenders

From new 2935 renumbered 100	
13/3/47	110
3/9/55	118
16/11/55	106
28/1/57	115

Mileage at 28/12/63 733,933
Withdrawn 6/7/64

COUNTY OF MIDDLESEX at Old Oak shed, 4 February 1956. This is the original 'draughting experiment' double chimney it had from new. It was distinctively different from the double chimney derived from 1009's trials with its tin chimney, possessing as it did this prominent lip. The 'standard' double chimney did not have this lip; one was fitted to 1000 early in 1958 so that all the Counties in the end had the same chimney arrangement. Peter Groom.

Left, below. 1000 with its standard chimney, getting ready with a freight in the early 1960s. In private correspondence R.C. Riley, with a finely attuned appreciation of GWR 4-6-0s and a practical experience of their working capabilities, described the Counties as 'controversial', a reference perhaps to the heavy hammer blow of the two cylinder locos and the abandonment of proven Churchward features such as the de Glehn bogie. www.rail-online.co.uk

1001 COUNTY OF BUCKS

To traffic 12/9/45
Named 12/47

Mileage and boilers

From new		9901
8/12/47	97,693	9901
9/8/49	173,553	C9908
21/5/51	256,036	C992?
9/10/53	348,863	C9905
1/11/55	430,222	C9905
23/10/56	458,590	C9914
20/12/57	503,740	C9907
22/11/60	587,278	C????

? part of original GWR History Sheet missing
at The National Archive

Sheds and Works

1/12/45	Newton Abbot
15/10/45	Swindon Works **R**
31/12/45	Newton Abbot Shed **R**
25/4/46	Newton Abbot Shed **R**
19/11/46	Newton Abbot Works **L**
23/4/47	Newton Abbot Shed **R**
8/12/47	Swindon Works **I**
4/9/46	Neyland
19/4/49	Carmarthen Shops **U**
9/8/49	Swindon Works **HG**
13/12/49	Llanelly Shops **U**
15/4/50	Llanelly Shops **U**
24/8/50	Llanelly Shops **U**
16/10/50	Llanelly Shops **U**
26/1/51	Neyland Shops **U**
21/5/51	Swindon Works **HG**
8/9/52	Swindon Works **U**
9/10/53	Swindon Works **HG**
13/8/54	Swindon Works **LC**
8/11/54	Neyland Shops **U**
1/11/55	Swindon Works **HI**
29/12/55*	Caerphilly Works **LC**
23/10/56	Swindon Works **HC**
5/11/56	Swindon Works **U**
20/12/57	Swindon Works **HG**
8/5/58	Carmarthen Shops **U**
9/2/59	Swindon Works **HC**
22/11/60	Swindon Works **HI**
2/1/61	Swindon Works **HI cont**
28/1/61	Penzance
6/10/62	Neyland

*First visit of a County – detained for
attention to superheater header until 4/1/56

Tenders

From new	2936 renumbered 101
13/6/49	111
27/8/53	101
30/12/57	119

Final recorded mileage 664,361
Withdrawn 24/5/63

1001 running without nameplates, at Exeter St David's with a down stopping train on 26 September 1946. *The Railway Observer* usefully provides a snapshot of County activity in 1946; by March they were working all the principal routes from Paddington and 1001, 1004 and 1006 were working regularly into Penzance. R.C. Riley, transporttreasury.co.uk

1001 spent its life in the west – of Wales and England. Most of that life it worked from Neyland shed, starting out at Newton Abbot but making the move to Wales after only a year or so. It came to Penzance only at the beginning of 1961 and went away again the following year to – Neyland. Here it is at Penzance during its 'English' period. It would not have been seen at Paddington a lot, for engines off through working from West Wales came off at Swansea. All big WR engines were repaired at Swindon, so Neyland 4-6-0s could, with luck, be seen on running in turns at Paddington. Llandore, moreover, ran Castles to London and could borrow engines from further west if pushed but it was like seeing the occasional Haymarket engine at Kings Cross. J. Leaf, colourrail.co.uk

1001 at an unknown date, though it is before the fitting of a double chimney at the end of 1957. 1001 is at Swindon Factory, positioned in front of the AW wheel shop. This was the most westerly in the 'A' shop complex; on the extreme left are wheelsets awaiting attention in the shop. transporttreasury.co.uk

Laira shed on 27 January 1962 and Penzance's 1001 COUNTY OF BUCKS in fine condition is up for the match. Plymouth Argyle were playing Tottenham Hotspur that day and (presumably) has brought up supporters from the west. The Spurs supporters had come down behind at least three Kings which were lined up for attention on the far side of the coal stage. Other excursions had been run from Broxbourne in Hertfordshire, Spurs-supporter territory, in part at least double headed by Castles – one of them, 4087 stands to the right. Behind are the Type 4s which will very soon be numerous enough to largely eliminate the GW 4-6-0s. By the following year for instance, a couple of Laira Counties were still working in the West but three of them were in store at the shed. Peter W. Gray.

1002 COUNTY OF BERKS

To traffic 27/9/45
Named 5/47

Mileages and Boilers

From new		9902
24/3/49	165,696	C9951
11/10/50	246,963	C9926
12/9/52	333,631	C9906
9/11/53	391,743	C9904
2/2/55	446,720	C9951
31/10/56	526,340	C9951
4/6/58	587,279	C9917
23/1/61	693,775	C9911

Sheds and Works

1/12/45	Bath Road
21/5/47	Swindon Works **I**
18/6/47	Didcot Shops **R**
2/6/48	Bath Road Shops **L**
	Tender Work only
24/3/49	Swindon Works **HG**
28/3/50	Newton Abbot Shed **Cas**
11/10/50	Swindon Works **HG**
4/12/50	Swindon Works **U**
11/1/51	Bath Road Shops **U**
17/7/52	Laira Shops **U**
12/9/52	Swindon Works **HI**
21/3/53	Laira
8/4/53	Swindon Works **U**
16/5/53	Penzance
9/11/53	Swindon Works **HC**
2/2/55	Swindon Works **HG**
5/1/56	Penzance Shops **U**
31/10/56	Swindon Works **HI**
22/6/57	Penzance Shops **U**
25/11/57	Newton Abbot Works **LC**

4/6/58	Swindon Works **HG**
30/4/59	Swindon Works **HI**
18/6/60	St. Blazey
5/11/60	Laira
3/12/60	Penzance
23/1/61	Swindon Works **HG**
25/2/61	Didcot
18/5/61	Swindon Works **LI**

Transferred to LMR book stock 30/12/62*

3/11/62	Shrewsbury
7/6/63	Banbury Shops **U**

*The 'Great Transfer' of WR sheds in Areas 84 Wolverhampton and 89 Shrewsbury took formal effect, it seems, from 1/1/63. The actual re-codings did not come into force until 9/9/63, with the formation of the 2 Tyseley and 6 Chester Divisions. It made little operational difference for it was already a matter of managing steam's extinction over the succeeding couple of years or so.

Tenders

From new	2927 renumbered 102
18/9/50	125
4/2/58	105
24/4/59	104
11/1/61	111

'Reputedly running with coal-weighing tender 4125' in July 1954

Final recorded mileage 766,263
Withdrawn 17/9/63

At Snow Hill, Saturday 5 August 1961 with the 9.45am Paddington-Wrexham, by now a scruffy Didcot engine. Michael Mensing.

1002 COUNTY OF BERKS arriving at Par station on Whit Monday, 18 May 1959, with the up Cornishman. Double chimney fitted the previous year. Michael Mensing.

Fresh off works at Swindon shed on 3 May 1959, ready for return to Penzance. Very soon it would move on to St Blazey. A.W. Battson, transporttreasury.co.uk

The 12 noon Penzance to Manchester and Glasgow, leaving Treverrin tunnel near Lostwithiel, 13 June 1956. Michael Mensing.

1003 COUNTY OF WILTS

To traffic 2/10/45
Named 8/47

Mileages and Boilers

From new		9903
9/8/47	81,660	C9908
2/5/49	164,273	C9952
8/2/51	256,113	C9906
8/8/52	311,650	C9909
19/3/54	378,329	C9924
22/2/56	449,152	C9954
8/11/57	510,872	C9912
26/5/60	583,872	C9908

Sheds and Works

9/12/45	Swindon Works **R**
29/12/45	Old Oak
8/8/46	Newton Abbot Shed **R**
21/9/46	Old Oak Shops **R**
11/2/47	Laira Shops **R**
9/8/47	Swindon Works **I**
7/7/48	Swindon Works **L**
2/5/49	Swindon Works **HG**
5/1/50	Swindon Works **U**
8/4/50	Bath Road Shops **U**
20/9/50	Old Oak shops **U**
13/10/50	Old Oak Shed **LC**
30/12/50	Laira
8/2/51	Swindon Works **HG**
21/4/51	Shrewsbury
8/8/52	Swindon Works **HI**
19/3/54	Swindon Works **HG**
30/9/55	Tyseley Shops **U**
22/2/56	Swindon Works **HI**
12/4/56	Shrewsbury Shops **U**
8/11/57	Swindon Works **HG**
26/11/57	Didcot Shops **U**
13/6/58	Shrewsbury Shops **U**
28/1/59	Stafford Road Shed **U**
24/6/59	Wolverhampton Works **HC**
20/10/59	Old Oak Shops **LC**
26/5/60	Swindon Works **HI**
28/1/61	Laira
1/9/61	Wolverhampton Works **HC**
27/1/62	Laira Shops **U**
15/7/62	Gloucester Shops **U**
8/8/62	Laira Shops **U**

Tenders

From new	2938 renumbered 103
29/9/56	113
26/5/60	128

Final recorded mileage 655,000
Withdrawn 22/10/62

1003 COUNTY OF WILTS at Shrewsbury shed, 26 September 1954. It had been one of the original Old Oak Counties, finding its way to Shrewsbury via a brief stint at Laira. Colourrail.co.uk

32

At Cardiff General in fine external condition, 30 August 1956; across the platform, perhaps surprisingly, sits a WD 2-8-0. Stephen Gradidge.

1003 COUNTY OF WILTS at Newton Abbot shed on 19 July 1958, still a Shrewsbury engine, off one of those heroic north-south jobs. R.C. Riley, transporttreasury.co.uk

Swindon on 3 November 1957, on the occasion of a Heavy General, with its newly-acquired double chimney. 1003's official release came some days later and after trials and running in it went back to Shrewsbury after a few weeks. The running in involved some minor out-of-course repairs/adjustments at Didcot. Stephen Gradidge.

Interesting weathering of black livery on 1003 at Bath Road shed, 1 August 1953. Norman Preedy Archive.

1003 withdrawn but still looking pretty much ready for the road, at Laira shed, 7 April 1963. The view is useful to show the reverser, normally obscured by the right-hand nameplate, which on this side had to have its own supporting plate. Two casings now on right-hand side, indicating increased superheat. Peter Groom

1004 COUNTY OF SOMERSET

To traffic 15/10/45
Named 8/46

Mileages and boilers

From new		9904
12/9/47	81,485	C9903
4/10/49	166,465	C9911
15/6/51	247,217	C9908
20/4/53	321,345	C9911
17/3/55	408,322	C9912
17/4/57	489,217	C9952
24/12/59	578,426	C9903

Sheds and Works

29/12/45	Laira
9/5/46	Penzance Shops **R**
9/8/46	Laira Shops **R**
12/9/47	Swindon Works **I**
1/7/48	Newton Abbot Works **I**
	Tender work only
16/2/49	Laira Shops **U**
24/7/49	Laira Shops **U**
54/10/49	Swindon Works **HG**
21/6/50	Penzance Shops **U**
7/11/50	Penzance Shops **U**
4/4/51	Penzance Shops **U**
15/6/51	Swindon Works **HI**
1/12/51	Shrewsbury
25/7/52	Shrewsbury Shops **U**
3/2/53	Shrewsbury Shops **U**

21/2/53	Stafford Road
20/4/53	Swindon Works **HG**
8/5/53	Swindon Works **U**
27/2/54	Swindon
24/7/54	Reading Shops **U**
17/3/55	Swindon Works **HI**
24/5/55	Swindon Shed **U**
25/4/56	Old Oak Shops **U**
17/4/57	Swindon Works **HG**
28/10/58	Swindon Works **LC**
24/12/59	Swindon Works **HI**
6/7/60	Swindon Shed **U**
31/12/60	Penzance
19/2/62	Penzance Shops **U**
29/6/62	Penzance Shops **LC**
2/8/62	Penzance Shops **U**

Tenders

From new	2939 renumbered 104
16/2/52	119
15/2/55	100
17/4/57	110
24/12/59	114

Final recorded mileage 657,523
Withdrawn 21/9/62

That distinctive front end at Swindon shed on 30 January 1955. As stated somewhere else, look at the front end of a County and allow your eyes to un-focus slightly and an 8F emerges... See, indeed, page 1. Pannier tank 5741 in background.

On the same spot four years later, in May 1959; they didn't change much... The main alteration of course is the double chimney, though the tender emblem has changed too. The tender has the white ash deposit, usually an unfortunate side effect of 'paddling' the fire from the cab; the Counties had hopper ashpans but not rocking grates; this one carries the BR 'SC' plate under the shedplate indicating the (theoretical) presence of ash sieves in the smokebox... Norman Preedy Archive.

Head of an impressive line-up at Laira shed on 22 April 1962. Rest of the coaled-up engines are 5065, 5024, three Halls and Small Prairie 4561. Terry Nicholls.

Single chimney 1004 COUNTY OF SOMERSET turning on the boarded-over turntable at Reading shed, 21 June 1955. Typical GW spare lamp on extra irons by left-hand cylinder. A.R. Carpenter, transporttreasury.co.uk

1005 COUNTY OF DEVON

To traffic 6/11/45
Named 7/46

Mileages and Boilers

From new		9905
15/10/47	83,617	C9904
16/8/49	172,498	C9914
18/5/51	258,398	C9907
11/3/53	345,980	C9927
12/1/55	419,228	C9920
26/10/56	505,743	C9920
12/12/58	569,203	C9900
16/9/60	636,600	C9900
16/7/62	680,939	C9926

Sheds and Works

29/12/45	Bath Road
19/6/46	Swindon Works Balancing
11/7/46	Swindon Works **R**
24/7/46	Swindon Works **R**
31/7/47	Swindon Works **R**
15/10/47	Swindon Works **I**
4/3/48	Swindon Works **R**
16/8/49	Swindon Works **HG**
18/5/51	Swindon Works **HI**
7/3/52	Taunton Shops **U**
18/5/52	Swindon Shed **LC**

11/3/53	Swindon Works **HG**
11/12/53	Swindon Works **LC**
11/4/54	Exeter Shops **U**
12/1/55	Swindon Works **HG**
26/10/56	Swindon Works **HI**
12/10/57	Newton Abbot Works **LC**
12/12/58	Swindon Works **HG**
9/1/59	Old Oak Shops **U**
16/10/59	Swindon Shed **U**
10/9/60	St. Philips Marsh
16/9/60	Caerphilly Works **HI**
3/7/61	Ebbw Jct. Shops **U**
17/10/61	Old Oak Shops **U**
18/4/62	Hereford Shops **U**
16/7/62	Swindon Works **HC**

Tenders

From new	2940 renumbered 105
20/8/58	129
12/12/58	108
22/7/62	116

Final recorded mileage 710,034
Withdrawn 24/6/63

1005 COUNTY OF DEVON at home at Bristol Bath Road, being readied for a job up to London perhaps. It was here for some fifteen years, from new, until dieselisation work meant the entire complement was consigned to St Philips Marsh. Among many others, Castles and so on, no fewer then eight Counties moved the short distance to 'The Marsh' from 10 September 1960: 1000, 1005, 1009, 1011, 1014, 1024, 1027 and 1028, never to return. That front footstep suggests that stouter staff were at a disadvantage...

Single chimney 1005 COUNTY OF DEVON at Taunton. J Robertson, transporttreasury.co.uk

With double chimney at Shrewsbury shed; second tender emblem, increased superheat. J Robertson, transporttreasury.co.uk

1005 passing Penzance shed with an up train of empty stock, 11 May 1959. Michael Mensing.

1006 COUNTY OF CORNWALL

To traffic 15/11/45
Named 4/48

Mileages and Boilers

From new		9906
22/4/48	88,272	C9950
8/12/50	193,560	C9920
30/1/53	274,081	C9920
5/10/54	350,044	C9903
17/1/57	440,876	C9905
9/12/58	538,601	C9913
16/12/60	611,968	C9951

Sheds and Works

29/12/45	Laira
29/3/46	Laira Shops **R**
29/8/46	Laira Shops **R**
19/1/46	Laira Shops **R**
22/5/47	Laira Shops **R**
24/6/47	Laira Shops **R**
31/10/47	Newton Abbot Works **L**
	Tender work only
22/4/48	Swindon Works **I**
8/10/48	Newton Abbot Works **L**
	Tender work only
18/5/49	Laira Shops **U**
22/7/49	Laira Shops **U**
14/9/49	Laira Shops **U**
21/11/49	Swindon Works **LC**
30/12/49	Penzance Shops **U**
7/6/50	Laira shops **U**
8/12/50	Swindon Works **HG**
18/3/51	Laira Shops **U**
22/1/52	Laira shops **U**
15/2/52	Old Oak Shops **U**
24/3/52	Laira Shops **U**
26/5/52	Laira Shops **U**
27/6/52	Laira Shops **U**
18/9/52	Laira Shops **U**
30/1/53	Swindon Works **HI**
10/9/53	Laira Shops **U**
7/10/53	Laira Shops **U**
30/12/53	Laira shops **U**
19/6/54	Carmarthen
6/11/54	Penzance
5/10/54	Swindon Works **HG**
16/7/55	Truro
5/11/55	Penzance
5/12/55	Swindon Shed **LC**
25/5/56	Newton Abbot Works **LC**
17/1/57	Swindon Works **HI**
6/8/58	Penzance Shops **U**
9/12/58	Swindon Works **HG**
18/6/60	St. Blazey
5/11/60	Laira
16/12/60	Swindon Works **HI**
6/9/61	Laira Shops **U**
24/1/62	Swindon Works **HC**
22/5/62	Laira Shops **U**
29/6/62	Wolverhampton Works **HC**
15/12/62	Swindon

Tenders

From new	2941 renumbered 106
5/12/55	108
9/12/58	100
10/12/60	127

Final recorded mileage 687,685
Withdrawn 17/9/63

1006 COUNTY OF CORNWALL at Lostwithiel 14 June 1956 on the 11.5am Plymouth-Penzance. Michael Mensing.

At Exeter St David's, still with single chimney, August 1957. J. Robertson, transporttreasury.co.uk

With the down Cornishman at Truro, 20 May 1959. Michael Mensing.

1006 COUNTY OF CORNWALL (it had come new to Laira) climbing to Treverrin tunnel, south of Lostwithiel, with the 3.40pm Plymouth-Penzance, 13 June 1956. Michael Mensing.

1007 COUNTY OF BRECKNOCK

To traffic 5/12/45
Named 1/48

Mileages and boilers

From new		9907
12/1/48	89,390	C9910
3/11/49	181,155	C9905
3/8/51	262,069	C9901
5/10/53	357,430	C9954
4/8/55	427,355	C9902
17/5/57	492,853	C9903
10/12/59	583,436	C9922

Sheds and Works

29/12/45	Bath Road
9/9/46	Laira Shops **R**
6/12/46	Bath Road Shops **R**
4/11/47	Newton Abbot Works **R**
12/1/48	Swindon Works **I**
25/1/49	Swindon Works **U**
3/11/49	Swindon Works **HG**
5/11/50	Taunton shops **U**
8/12/50	Swindon Works **U**
3/8/51	Swindon Works **HI**
11/9/52	Swindon Works **LC**
20/12/52	Reading Shops **U**
5/10/53	Swindon Works **HG**
12/12/54	Swindon Works **LC**
29/1/55	Truro
4/8/55	Swindon Works **HI**
17/5/57	Swindon Works **HG**
5/7/57	Swindon Works **U**
2/10/57	Swindon Works **U**
3/10/59	Exeter
10/12/59	Swindon Works **HG**
25/3/61	Didcot
15/9/61	Swindon Works **HC**

Tenders

From new	2942 renumbered 107
14/5/55	114
17/5/57	127
10/12/59	103

Final recorded mileage 658,967
Withdrawn 5/10/62

1007 COUNTY OF BRECKNOCK, in lined black, receiving attention at Truro shed; NOT TO BE MOVED warning on the tender.

COUNTY OF BRECKNOCK at Swindon Works, probably at the end of 1953 after its Heavy General that year. On the footplate are various bits of old timber, for the loco's imminent lighting-up. www.rail-online.co.uk

1007 COUNTY OF BRECKNOCK with new double chimney, making its way out of Penzance station and heading for Long Rock shed, July 1957.

Double chimney 1007 at work in the West (it was at Truro for most of the latter half of the 1950s) with the 4.15pm Truro-Penzance, climbing to the summit between Truro and Chacewater on 28 November 1959. Michael Mensing.

In the ancient confines of Shrewsbury shed, about 1959. M.L. Boakes.

1007 passing Silverton with an up express, 18 July 1959. R.C. Riley, transporttreasury.co.uk

With an up express to Paddington at Cowley Bridge, 16 July 1960. R.C. Riley, transporttreasury.co.uk

In black at Truro shed, 26 September 1956. H.C. Casserley, courtesy R.M. Casserley.

1008 COUNTY OF CARDIGAN

To traffic 10/12/45
Named 6/47

Mileages and boilers

From new		9908
13/6/47	74,951	R9931
25/2/49	168,627	C9922
14/12/50	257,718	C9923
20/8/52	342,102	C9903
9/7/54	414,719	C9909
15/10/56	501,674	C9909
28/5/58	550,493	C9928
21/8/59	600,301	C9918
9/11/61	672,081	C9902

Sheds and Works

26/1/46	Old Oak
27/11/46	Laira **R**
27/1/47	Old Oak Shed **I**
13/6/47	Swindon Works **I**
27/2/48	Old Oak Shed **R**
9/11/48	Old Oak Shops **R**
25/2/49	Swindon Works **HG**
31/10/49	Old Oak Shops **U**
2/3/50	Swindon Works **LC**
23/6/50	Swindon Works **LC**
14/12/50	Swindon Works **HG**
5/4/51	Ebbw Jct. Shops **U**
18/6/51	Old Oak Shops **U**
20/8/52	Swindon Works **HI**
1/11/52	Chester
5/6/53	Wolverhampton Works **LC**
14/5/54	Wolverhampton Works **U**

9/7/54	Swindon Works **HG**
29/9/54	Leamington Spa Shops **U**
15/10/56	Swindon Works **HI**
Transferred to LMR book stock 23/2/58*	
28/5/58	Swindon Works **HG**
Returned to WR book stock 15/6/58	
15/6/58	Penzance
9/8/58	Laira
7/10/58	Laira Shops **U**
21/1/59	Penzance
21/8/59	Swindon Works **HG**
26/10/60	Penzance Shops **U**
9/11/61	Swindon Works **HG**
6/10/62	Neyland
Transferred to LMR book stock 24/2/63**	
23/3/63	Shrewsbury
1/5/63	Shrewsbury Shops **U**
3/9/63	Shrewsbury shops **U**
29/9/63	Swindon

*Chester shed transferred to LMR
**See note under 1002

Tenders

From new	2943 renumbered 108
8/7/52	126
31/5/54	124

Final recorded mileage 726,835
Withdrawn 3/10/63

COUNTY OF CARDIGAN back at Chester around 1963; it carries the 89A plate of Shrewsbury, before the shed was transferred to the LMR. www.rail-online.co.uk

Chester's 1008 COUNTY OF CARDIGAN in workaday condition at Canton shed, Cardiff on 13 September 1953. The Counties had sanding to the front of the leading driver and to the rear of the trailing one. The sandbox, with filler cap, for the latter was mounted under the cab while the front sandbox was hidden away behind the slidebars, its filler cap barely visible on the running plate. Norman Preedy Archive.

1008 COUNTY OF CARDIGAN, a Penzance engine by now, with the 4.50pm Penzance-Manchester, beginning the descent from Chacewater to Truro, 16 May 1959. Michael Mensing.

Still a Shrewsbury (89A) loco, 1008 COUNTY OF CARDIGAN leaves Gobowen for Shrewsbury in 1963. Goods trains became a common source of work for Counties towards the end. P. Ward.

1009 COUNTY OF CARMARTHEN

To traffic 21/12/45
Named 2/48

Mileages and Boilers

From new		9909
6/2/48	88,746	C9917
14/4/49	139,978	C9928
14/2/52	275,444	C9917
1/6/54	360,863	C9919
19/9/56	457,859	C9919
23/9/58	545,841	C9909
11/5/60	619,521	C9916
30/10/61	666,407	C9921

Sheds and Works

26/1/46	Laira
7/9/46	Laira Shops **R**
6/10/46	Laira Shops **R**
3/12/46	Laira Shops **R**
9/2/47	Laira Shops **R**
14/4/47	Newton Abbot Works **L**
19/7/47	Laira Shops **R**
31/10/47	Newton Abbot Works **L**
	Tender work only
6/2/48	Swindon Works **I** *W suffix*
6/8/48	Laira Shops **R**
4/9/48	Neyland
23/11/48	Llanelly Shops **L**
14/4/49	Swindon Works **HC**
31/3/50	Swindon Works **HI**
24/3/51	Neyland Shops **U**
14/2/52	Swindon Works **HG**
15/6/53	Llanelly Shops **U**

1/6/54	Swindon Works **HG**
26/7/54	Swindon Works
	Experimental Work
9/11/54	Swindon Works **U**
	Hot box
29/12/54	Swindon Works
	Ex-Test Plant
7/1/55	Swindon Works **LC**
29/1/55	Bath Road
19/9/56	Swindon Works **HI**
28/8/57	Old Oak Shops **U**
18/5/58	Laira Shops **U**
23/9/58	Swindon Works **HG**
30/10/59	Newton Abbot Works **LC**
11/5/60	Swindon Works **HI**
10/9/60	St. Philips Marsh
3/1/61	Westbury Shops **U**
23/2/61	St. Philips Marsh Shops **U**
30/10/61	Swindon Works **HC**
30/4/62	Swindon Works **HC**
23/1/63	Taunton shops **U**

Tenders

From new	2944 renumbered 109
23/9/58	128
11/5/60	113
30/4/62	112

Final recorded mileage 702,148
Withdrawn 1/2/63

Yet to be named, 1009 rests in a siding at Laira, its home shed, on 22 June 1947. Forward washout plug cover hanging loose.
R.C. Riley, transporttreasury.co.uk

Now a Bristol Bath Road engine, 1009 COUNTY OF CARMARTHEN has turned at Ranelagh Bridge outside Paddington ready for return to Bristol on 30 March 1957, lamp on for the run into the terminus, just beyond the girders of the eponymous bridge in the background. The round trip could be accomplished on one tender of coal, and there was no supply available at Ranelagh. For once it's possible to examine the fitment of the reporting number bracket; it sits on and is secured to the smokebox darts, it turns out. Self-cleaning smokebox 'SC' plate on smokebox door. R.C. Riley, transporttreasury.co.uk

By now a St Philips Marsh engine, 1009 COUNTY OF CARMARTHEN at Swindon shed on 12 August 1962; the class was still intact, just, but withdrawals would commence in a few weeks. 1009 itself had only a few months left at work. Stephen Gradidge.

1010 COUNTY OF CAERNARVON

To traffic 22/1/46
Named 12/47 COUNTY OF CARNARVON; plates altered 11/51

Mileages and Boilers

From new		9910
16/12/47	87,762	C9901
6/12/49	179,084	C9918
15/11/51	264,339	C9904
24/9/53	357,847	C9902
1/7/55	438,053	C9904
25/1/57	523,891	C9911
9/1/59	624,880	C9911
8/7/60	675,110	C9912
29/11/61	721,519	C9919

Sheds and Works

23/2/46	Old Oak
14/3/46	Swindon Works **R**
17/5/46	Newton Abbot Works **L**
19/4/47	Westbury Shops **R**
14/8/47	Old Oak shops **L**
16/12/47	Swindon Works **I**
30/4/48	Laira Shops **I**
22/7/49	Old Oak Shed **U**
19/8/49	Laira Shops **U**
6/12/49	Swindon Works **HG**
13/3/50	Old Oak Shops **U**
2/6/50	Old Oak Shops **U**
30/12/50	Laira
3/4/51	Old Oak Shops **U**
18/5/51	Laira Shops **U**
22/6/51	Taunton Shops **U**
3/8/51	Taunton Shops **U**
15/11/51	Swindon Works **HG**
1/8/52	Laira Shops **U**
31/10/52	Laira Shops **U**
22/1/53	Swindon Works **LC**
24/9/53	Swindon Works **HG**
28/7/54	Laira Shops **U**
24/2/55	Laira Shops **U**
27/4/55	Laira Shops **U**
1/7/55	Swindon Works **HG**
15/6/56	Swindon Works **LC**
25/1/57	Swindon Works **HG**
31/10/57	Newton Abbot Works **LC**
30/1/58	Swindon Works **HC**
30/9/58	Laira Shops **U**
9/1/59	Swindon Works **HI**
3/10/59	Swindon
11/12/59	Newton Abbot Works **LC**
8/7/60	Swindon Works **HG**
29/11/61	Swindon Works **HG**
20/11/62	Old Oak Shops **U**

Tenders

From new	2945 renumbered 110
24/11/52	101
21/8/53	111
19/5/55	107
18/6/56	128
25/1/57	107
29/11/61	106

Mileage as at 28/12/63 779,055
Withdrawn 24/7/64

Single chimney 1010 COUNTY OF CAERNARVON, Cornish Riviera headboard up, at home shed Laira in the summer of 1954.
J. Robertson, transporttreasury.co.uk

Newly overhauled at Swindon Works, 22 June 1955; after a week or two it will be ready to return to Laira. This would be its first application of BR lined dark green. Norman Preedy Archive.

COUNTY OF CAERNARVON at home at Laira, February 1956; bogie out for attention, tender necessarily uncoupled for the 'lift' of the loco. www.rail-online.co.uk

1010 COUNTY OF CAERNARVON leaving Plymouth North Road with the up Cornishman, 4 July 1957. A Southern mogul has a train of vans on the left. R.C. Riley, transporttreasury.co.uk

1010 on the sea wall at Teignmouth, in the summer of 1957; it had got its double chimney at the beginning of the year and the exigencies of the summer peak have doubtless contributed to it running without the cover to the safety valves! In fact there was a spate of absent bonnets around this time, even with Kings. It has been blamed on a disaffected fitter, working to rule. J. Robertson, transporttreasury.co.uk

By now a Swindon engine (it would spend its final years there) 1010 looks work-weary stabled alongside an unknown shed. It's a guess, but the building might even be the Newton Abbot 'Factory'. 1010 was there at the end of 1959, shortly after its transfer to Swindon and it has had some work; the rods have been cleaned up, indicating their removal recently and '1010' is chalked on the bogie, while various 'bits' sit on the running plate. www.rail-online.co.uk

At Old Oak on 5 June 1963; twin casings on smokebox. Peter Groom.

1011 COUNTY OF CHESTER

To traffic 29/1/46
Named 11/47

Mileages and Boilers

From new		9911
13/11/47	81,520	C9912
11/10/49	172,074	C9904
2/7/51	258,004	C9954
13/5/53	346,056	C9907
24/1/55	411,119	C9915
29/3/57	497,221	C9923
5/11/58	576,435	C9924
29/6/61	661,525	C9924
9/11/62	694,084	C9910

Sheds and Works

23/2/46	Bath Road
25/7/46	Bath Road Shops **R**
13/11/47	Swindon Works **I**
24/6/48	Ebbw Jct. Shops **R**
18/10/48	Taunton Shops **R**
28/4/49	Newton Abbot Shed **U**
11/10/49	Swindon Works **HG**
25/10/50	Bath Road Shops **U**
2/7/51	Swindon Works **HI**
9/6/52	Swindon Works **LC**
13/5/53	Swindon Works **HG**
15/1/54	Swindon Works **LC**
24/1/55	Swindon Works **HG**
28/3/56	Swindon Works **LC**
15/2/57	Penzance Shops **U**
29/3/57	Swindon Works **HI**
5/11/58	Swindon Works **HG**
26/4/60	Swindon Works **HC**
10/9/60	St. Philips Marsh
20/1/61	Caerphilly Works **LC**
29/6/61	Wolverhampton Works **LI**
14/3/62	Swindon Works **LC**
9/11/62	Swindon Works **HG**
30/11/63	Swindon
18/8/64	Worcester Shops **U**

Tenders

From new	2947, renumbered 112
10/11/54	110
29/2/57	100
5/10/58	109

Mileage as at 28/12/63 728,610
Withdrawn 11/64

1011 COUNTY OF CHESTER in classic view from the footbridge at Canton shed, Cardiff, 26 July 1952. A glimpse for once of the front filler sand filler cap, anonymous on the running plate; the front sandbox itself is barely visible behind the slidebars. R.C. Riley, transporttreasury.co.uk

A completely filthy 1011, the grime remarkable for its entirely uniform covering. Not a square inch is spared!

The first withdrawals, 1004, 1018 and 1026, came in September 1962 from widely different sheds, Penzance, Didcot and Shrewsbury. It nevertheless took over two years to eliminate the Counties, mainly because of the longevity of 1011 COUNTY OF CHESTER, which survived the rest by several months. Because of this it was in demand for railtours, with its number restored in block style to the bufferbeam. This is Swindon and the tour would be the SLS 'Last County Special' of 20 September 1964 from Birmingham Snow Hill and back again. 1011 was withdrawn a couple of months later.

That's better. Shimmering in green at Swindon shed; the photograph is undated but, given the BR dark green, the single chimney and right-facing emblem, in all likelihood the occasion is its Heavy Intermediate in March 1957. Full repaints were not always confined to Heavy Generals. Norman Preedy.

1012 COUNTY OF DENBIGH

To traffic 5/2/46
Named 7/46

Mileages and Boilers

From new		9912
31/10/47	88,861	C9905
30/8/49	184,178	C9907
30/1/51	266,349	C9952
15/12/52	355,986	C9923
13/8/54	448,964	C9950
23/12/55	522,934	C9950
10/9/57	608,742	C9902
23/12/60	726,446	C9917

Sheds and Works

23/2/46	Old Oak
3/7/46	Swindon Works **L**
19/3/47	Laira Shops **R**
23/5/47	Old Oak Shed **R**
31/10/47	Swindon Works **I**
16/4/48	Swindon Works **L**
6/9/48	Old Oak Shops **R**
21/4/49	Laira Shops **U**
30/8/49	Swindon Works **HG**
28/3/50	Old Oak Shops **U**
30/12/50	Laira
8/1/51	Taunton Shops **U**
31/1/51	Laira Shops **U**
30/3/51	Swindon Works **HI**
15/12/52	Swindon Works **HG**
20/4/53	Laira Shops **U**
27/1/54	Laira Shops **U**
11/6/54	Laira Shops **U**
13/8/54	Swindon Works **HG**
3/5/55	Laira Shops **U**
6/10/55	Laira Shops **U**
23/12/55	Swindon Works **HI**
6/10/56	Swindon
18/10/56	Laira Shops **U**
10/9/57	Swindon Works **HG**
3/12/57	Wolverhampton Works **HC**
21/3/58	Swindon Works **U**
5/9/58	Swindon Shed **LC**
27/11/59	Swindon Works **HC**
23/12/60	Swindon Works **HG**
24/3/62	Barrow Road Shed **U**
24/5/62	Wolverhampton Works **LC**
8/8/62	Reading Shops **U**
18/9/63	Gloucester Shed **U**
4/12/63	Swindon Shed **U**

Tenders

From new	2946, renumbered 111
6/7/49	101
14/11/52	127
21/12/55	121
27/11/49	127

Mileage as at 28/12/63 794,555
Withdrawn 24/4/64

Black-liveried 1012 COUNTY OF DENBIGH, at Laira shed on 3 September 1954. R.C. Riley, transporttreasury.co.uk

Neat in green at Milton, west of Didcot, 22 September 1961. This stopping train has a longer formation than many long distance services today. Michael Mensing.

Into the West. 1012 COUNTY OF DENBIGH, long a Laira engine, heads a train from Wolverhampton over the Royal Albert Bridge about teatime, 31 March 1952. A. Lathey, transporttreasury.co.uk

1013 COUNTY OF DORSET

To traffic 11/2/46
Named 1/47

Mileages and boilers

From new		9913
3/3/48	93,622	C9909
29/11/49	173,967	C9903
22/10/51	258,949	C9905
18/6/53	320,042	C9910
2/11/55	399,536	C9910
6/2/58	467,701	C9954
7/1/60	531,969	C9928
23/3/62	587,684	C9928

Sheds and Works

23/2/46	Bath Road
9/9/46	Taunton Shops **R**
4/1/47	Swindon Shops **L**
3/3/48	Swindon Works **I**
9/12/48	Swindon Works **L**
25/12/48	Laira
26/8/49	Laira Shops **U**
29/11/49	Swindon Works **HG**
22/4/50	Laira Shops **U**
20/5/50	Truro
10/3/51	Truro Shops **LC**
30/7/51	Truro Shops **U**
8/9/51	Penzance
22/10/51	Swindon Works **HI**
3/11/51	Stafford Road
1/12/51	Shrewsbury
9/9/52	Shrewsbury Shops **U**
13/5/53	Shrewsbury Shops **U**
18/6/53	Swindon Works **HG**
20/8/54	Swindon Works **LC**
20/9/54	Shrewsbury Shops **U**
21/4/55	Shrewsbury Shops **U**
19/9/55	Shrewsbury Shops **U**
2/11/55	Swindon Works **HI**
14/12/56	Wolverhampton Works **LC**
12/9/57	Swindon Works **LC**
6/2/58	Swindon Works **HG**
20/2/59	Swindon Works **LC**
7/1/60	Swindon Works **HG**
2/6/60	Shrewsbury Shops **U**
25/4/61	Oswestry Works **LC**
26/5/61	Shrewsbury Shops **U**
23/3/62	Swindon Works **HI**
9/11/62	Shrewsbury Shops **U**

Transferred to LMR book stock 30/12/62*

24/1/63	Wolverhampton Works **HC**
18/7/63	Wolverhampton Works **HC**

Transferred to WR book stock 8/9/63

29/9/63	Swindon

*See entry under 1002

Tenders

From new	2948 renumbered 113
29/9/56	103
7/4/60	123
23/3/62	129

Mileage at 28/12/63 630,737
Withdrawn 24/7/64

1013 COUNTY OF DORSET with double chimney, in green with electrification flashes, at Swindon in the 1960s; now with increased superheat. P. Chancellor, Colour-Rail

At its by-now home shed, Swindon, late April 1964. It is almost at the moment of its withdrawal. R.J. Buckley, Initial Photographics.

Late in life, a goods turn has brought Swindon's 1013 to Duffryn Yard shed, not a place often associated with Counties. rail-online

1014 COUNTY OF GLAMORGAN

To traffic 18/2/46
Named 3/48

Mileages and Boilers

From new		9914
15/3/48	78,217	C9913
14/12/49	165,535	C9912
5/9/51	248,006	C9911
3/3/53	317,934	C9952
2/3/55	389,271	C9952
6/11/56	466,703	C9928
23/8/58	544,997	C9916
18/2/60	635,205	C9952
7/7/62	712,396	C9927

Sheds and Works

23/2/46	Bath Road
13/3/46	Bath Road Shops **R**
27/4/46	Laira Shops **R**
2/5/47	Old Oak Shops **R**
11/7/47	Old Oak Shed **R**
6/12/47	Canton Shops **R**
29/1/48	Taunton Shops **R**
15/3/48	Swindon Works **I**
21/2/49	Old Oak shops **U**
20/7/49	Taunton Shops **U**
14/12/49	Swindon Works **HG**
8/11/50	Stafford Road Shops **U**
5/9/51	Swindon Works **HI**
4/9/52	Bath Road Shed **U**
26/11/52	Bath Road Shed **U**
3/3/53	Swindon Works **HG**
13/1/54	Swindon Works **LC**
7/5/54	Swindon Works **LC**
2/3/55	Swindon Works **HI**
6/11/56	Swindon Works **HG**
23/8/58	Swindon Works **HG**
18/2/60	Swindon Works **HI**
10/9/60	St. Philips Marsh
17/10/60	St. Philips Marsh Shops **U**
16/5/61	Swindon Works **HC**
7/10/61	Neyland
7/7/62	Swindon Works **HG**
Transferred to LMR book stock 24/3/63*	
19/4/63	Shrewsbury Shops **U**
20/4/63	Shrewsbury
10/6/63	Shrewsbury Shops **U**
Transferred to WR book stock 8/9/63	
29/9/63	Swindon
*See entry under 1002	

Tenders

From new	2949 renumbered 114
27/1/55	129
24/1/58	105
23/3/58	106
18/2/60	108
16/5/61	102

Trains Illustrated reports 1014 running with a Collett tender early December 1956. On 30 November 1014 had arrived at Paddington with a faulty tender – hot box perhaps – which made return home impossible. 1014 was escorted to Old Oak where Castle 5055 was in the Factory with its Collett tender 2847 lying idle. It was duly attached to 1014 which returned home. It was at least a couple of days before 1014 got its tender back, swapping over at Old Oak once again.

Mileage as at 28/12/63 756,762
Withdrawn 24/4/64

1014 may not be extinct for much longer! A new COUNTY OF GLAMORGAN is steadily taking shape – SEE: The County Project, Great Western Society, Didcot Railway Centre, Didcot, Oxfordshire.
Tel: +44 (0)1235 817200
drc@didcotrailwaycentre.co.uk

1014 COUNTY OF GLAMORGAN in GWR green with new ownership emblazoned in GW style, at Bristol Bath Road on 28 August 1948. H.C. Casserley, courtesy R.M. Casserley.

After its Heavy General in 1958; increased superheat appeared at this time. Behind are 2-8-0 3861 and Halls 5910 and 6907. M.L. Boakes.

Smokebox plate AWOL and replaced by a lily-livered paint version, on the Old Oak firepits on 16 September 1963. Alec Swain, transporttreasury.co.uk

The new County, arising from the mortal remains of a Modified Hall and an 8F, currently underway at Didcot, looks like being reincarnated as 1014 COUNTY OF GLAMORGAN: County Project, Great Western Society, Didcot Railway Centre, Didcot, Oxfordshire. Tel: +44 (0)1235 817200; drc@didcotrailwaycentre.co.uk

1014 COUNTY OF GLAMORGAN at Bristol Bath Road, this time in BR dark green, 3 March 1957. R.A. Panting.

1015 COUNTY OF GLOUCESTER

To traffic 1/3/46
Named 4/47

Mileages and Boilers

From new		9915
25/3/48	95,043	C9914
24/5/49	156,666	C9954*
31/8/51	248,663	C9951
23/4/53	350,748	C9951
10/11/54	417,743	C9926
6/7/56	504,547	C9913
25/11/58	587,358	C9920
6/10/60	662,672	C9920

First use of final boiler built for class

Sheds and Works

20/4/46	Old Oak
23/1/47	Old Oak Shops **R**
16/4/47	Swindon Works **L**
25/3/48	Swindon Works **I**
11/10/48	Old Oak Shops **R**
16/4/49	Taunton Shops **U**
24/5/49	Swindon Works **HG**
16/1/50	Old Oak Shops **U**
10/1/50	Bath Road Shops **U**
12/8/50	Oxford Shops **U**
20/12/50	Laira
20/2/51	Laira Shops **U**
31/8/51	Swindon Works **HG**
5/12/51	Laira Shops **U**
19/3/52	Laira Shops **U**
25/6/52	St. Blazey Shops **U**
30/9/52	Laira Shops **U**
23/4/53	Swindon Works **HI**
21/10/53	Swindon Works **LC**
9/11/53	Laira Shops **U**
3/6/54	Laira Shops **U**
10/11/54	Swindon Works **HG**
2/1/55	Laira Shops **U**
19/9/55	Swindon Works **LC**
26/3/56	Laira Shops **U**
6/7/56	Swindon Works **HI**
18/9/56	Laira Shops **U**
28/1/57	Swindon Works **LC**
16/11/57	Newton Abbot Works **LC**
5/12/57	Laira Shops **U**
1/1/58	Laira Shops **U**
25/11/58	Swindon Works **HG**
16/8/59	Laira Shops **U**
3/10/59	Swindon
10/1/60	Laira Shops **U**
6/10/60	Swindon Works **HI**
9/9/61	Didcot
5/4/62	Swindon Works **HC**
3/11/62	Laira, 'later withdrawn'*
12/11/62	Laira shops **U***

Conflicting entries which obviously mark the end of 1015. Early in 1963 it was still at Laira, dead (there wouldn't have been any repair, U or otherwise, surely) along with two other Counties, 1003 and 1004 awaiting disposal.

Tenders

From new	2950 renumbered 115
18/3/47	100
2/3/53	118
19/9/55	115
28/1/57	128
25/11/58	129
5/4/62	122

Final recorded mileage 724,192
Withdrawn 13/11/62

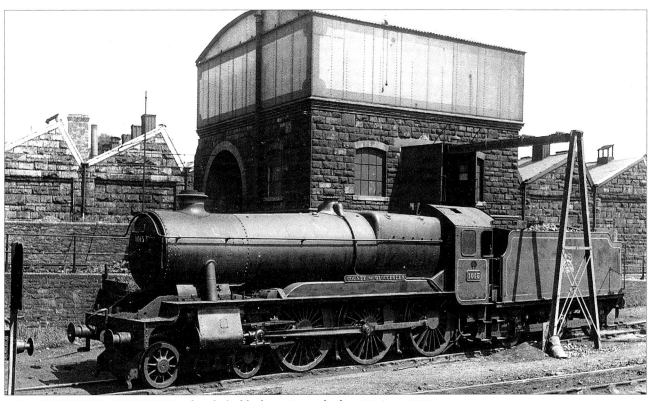

1015 COUNTY OF GLOUCESTER, already in black, at Truro shed on 24 June 1951.

1015 COUNTY OF GLOUCESTER in green, at Old Oak Common, 15 March 1959. The curious splasher recalled the unlamented failed aesthetics of the bullnose King and Castle. Both washout plug covers hanging loose and, considering how often these were left unfastened, it is a wonder they weren't removed altogether. Norman Preedy.

With an up express at Dawlish Warren, 15 July 1955. R.C. Riley, transporttreasury.co.uk

1015 COUNTY OF GLOUCESTER fresh out of works at Swindon after a Heavy Casual, on 1 April 1962. After the wheels and motion its main purpose seems to have been the fitting of enlarged superheater (hence the extra casing) and only the smokebox has been finished with a coat of paint. 81E Didcot shedplate. Alec Swain, transporttreasury.co.uk

At Oxford shed in June 1962. Colour-Rail.

In a livery of pure grey grime, 1015 comes into Temple Meads in 1961. rail-online

1016 COUNTY OF HANTS

To traffic 12/3/46
Named 9/46

Mileages and Boilers

From new		9916
19/4/48	80,670	C9915
18/1/50	155,874	C9910
26/9/51	228,749	C9912
12/2/53	289,276	C9916
2/12/54	356,087	C9923
7/3/57	426,656	C9927
22/4/59	511,557	C9901
21/7/61	577,158	C9905

Sheds and Works history

23/3/46	Stafford Road
3/8/46	Stafford Road Shed **R**
2/9/46	Swindon Works **R**
8/10/47	Oxford Shops **R**
4/12/47	Stafford Road Shed **L**
19/4/48	Swindon Works **I**
9/9/48	Stafford Road Shed **U**
21/10/49	Stafford Road Shed **U**
4/12/49	Laira shops **U**
18/1/50	Swindon Works **HG**
28/9/50	Stafford Road Shed **U**
5/1/51	Stafford Road Shed **U**
8/2/51	Tyseley Shops **U**
20/8/51	Reading Shops **U**

26/9/51	Swindon Works **HI**
21/12/51	Shrewsbury
23/2/52	Stafford Road
24/6/52	Oxford Shops **U**
1/11/52	Shrewsbury
12/2/53	Swindon Works **HI**
30/4/54	Shrewsbury **U**
11/10/54	Oxley Shops **U**
2/12/54	Swindon Works **HG**
21/12/54	Swindon Works **U**
	Hot box
4/11/55	Shrewsbury Shops **U**
7/3/56	Hereford Shops **U**
5/5/56	Shrewsbury Shops **U**
7/3/57	Swindon Works **HG**
28/5/59	Shrewsbury Shops **U***
22/4/59	Swindon Works **HG***
17/12/59	Wolverhampton Works **LC**
28/4/60	Shrewsbury Shops **U**
30/9/60	Shrewsbury shops **U**
21/7/61	Swindon Works **HG**
15/2/62	Wolverhampton Works **U**
10/7/62	Wolverhampton Works **U**

Listed in that order on History Sheet

Tenders

From new	2951 renumbered 116

Final recorded mileage 662,078
Withdrawn 17/9/63

Swindon shed, the spiritual home of the class it could almost seem, with 1016 COUNTY OF HANTS outside, about 1954.

1016 COUNTY OF HANTS with a train at Sutton Bridge Junction, Shrewsbury, about 1958. By now the whole of the class, or most of them, anyway (the 1959 Ian Allan *abc* still showed 280psi, altered to 250psi in the winter 1961 edition) had had the boiler pressure reduced to less elevated levels. 'This high pressure lark' as Dr Tuplin put it, was over. On the admittedly shaky basis of tractive effort, the Counties at 280psi were the most powerful two cylinder 4-6-0s in the country, exceeding that of the four cylinder Castles and closely approaching that of the three cylinder Royal Scots. www.rail-online.co.uk

1016 at Chester LMR shed – fairly late on from the increased superheat, denoted by the extra casing. Colour-Rail.

1017 COUNTY OF HEREFORD

To traffic 18/3/46
Named 3/46

Mileages and Boilers

Date	Mileage	Boiler
From new		9917
29/1/48	76,002	C9907
24/6/49	132,602	R9953
13/11/51	228,363	C9921
12/3/54	306,370	C9921
10/1/56	368,880	C9929
17/9/57	425,191	C9918
11/3/59	479,665	C9919
9/3/61	547,860	C9925

Sheds and Works

Date	Location	
20/4/46	Stafford Road	
15/11/46	Swindon Works	L
18/7/47	Stafford Road Shed	L
5/12/47	Slough Shops	R
29/1/48	Swindon Works	I *W suffix*
16/12/48	Wolverhampton Works	R
24/6/49	Swindon Works	HG
26/9/49	Wolverhampton Works	U
29/8/50	Swindon Works	LC
15/2/51	Croes Newydd Shops	U
23/5/51	Chester Shops	U
2/8/51	Banbury Shops	U
13/11/51	Swindon Works	HG
1/12/51	Shrewsbury	
7/2/52	Shrewsbury Shops	U
8/10/52	Shrewsbury Shops	U
23/2/53	Shrewsbury Shops	U
20/5/53	Wolverhampton Works	LC
12/3/54	Wolverhampton Works	HI
7/12/54	Tyseley Shops	U
21/5/55	Stafford Road	
18/4/55	Stafford Road Shed	U
22/9/55	Shrewsbury Shops	U
3/11/55	Wolverhampton Works	U
10/1/56	Swindon Works	HG
17/9/57	Swindon Works	HC
11/3/59	Swindon Works	HG
7/9/59	Caerphilly Works	LC
31/12/60	Laira	
28/1/61	Shrewsbury	
9/3/61	Swindon Works	HI
24/8/61	Ebbw Jct. Shops	U
30/1/62	Shrewsbury Shops	U
9/10/62	Shrewsbury Shops	?

Tenders

From new	2952 renumbered 117
9/3/61	108

Final recorded mileage 601,066
Withdrawn 19/12/62

1017 COUNTY OF HEREFORD with a down express, entering Totnes on 11 May 1954. Alan Lathey, transporttreasury.co.uk

Single chimney 1017 COUNTY OF HEREFORD in the first part of the 1950s, when it was a Shrewsbury engine. The location is the north end of Wolverhampton Low Level Station. 1017 went to Stafford Road when new but was later transferred to Shrewsbury. The over bridge carries the Wednesfield Road and the presence of trolley bus wires would date the photo around late 1950s. It would appear that 1017 is backing down to stock on the middle road. The bay on the side of the main down platform was used for stopping services to Shrewsbury. A. Robey, transporttreasury.co.uk

1017 COUNTY OF HEREFORD with a Birkenhead-Paddington train passing the site of Rhosrobin Halt, north of Wrexham on Easter Monday 18 April 1960. Michael Mensing.

1018 COUNTY OF LEICESTER

To traffic 23/3/46
Named 4/46

Mileages and Boilers

From new		9918
9/9/48	93,347	C9906
20/11/50	139,414	C9909
19/5/52	263,965	C9900
15/3/54	333,380	C9913
13/4/56	425,334	C9906
6/1/58	517,076	C9929
23/11/59	602,037	C9923

Sheds and Works

20/4/46	Newton Abbot
4/10/46	Newton Abbot Shed **R**
5/5/47	Swindon Works **L**
19/9/47	Newton Abbot Shed **R**
5/2/48	Newton Abbot Works **R**
24/6/48	Newton Abbot Works **L**
	Tender work only
9/9/48	Swindon Works **I**
27/7/49	Newton Abbot Works **LC**
13/10/49	Swindon Works **LC**
12/7/50	Gloucester Shops **U**
11/8/50	Newton Abbot Works **U**

20/11/50	Swindon Works **HG**
28/12/50	Penzance then Laira
9/3/51	Penzance Shops **U**
1/12/51	Shrewsbury
19/5/52	Swindon Works **HI**
27/12/52	Stafford Road
13/2/53	Wolverhampton Works **U**
10/7/53	Slough Shops **U**
16/10/53	Stafford Road Shed **U**
15/3/54	Swindon Works **HG**
11/9/54	Laira
14/9/54	Stafford Road Shed **U**
15/10/54	Truro Shops **U**
13/4/56	Swindon Works **HI**
6/1/58	Swindon Works **HG**
23/11/59	Swindon Works **HG**
18/6/60	Laira
3/12/60	Penzance
25/2/61	Didcot
5/10/61	Wolverhampton Works **U**

Tenders

From new	2953 renumbered 118
10/4/52	102
13/4/56	123
23/11/59	121

Final recorded mileage 680,979
Withdrawn 27/9/62

1018 COUNTY OF LEICESTER with The Royal Duchy passing St Germans in style on 30 May 1958. A Lathey, transporttreasury.co.uk

At Shrewsbury with the 1.40pm Birkenhead-Paddington, 23 June 1962. Extra casing on right-hand side but of a different outline to ones seen earlier. Norman Preedy

The days on The Royal Duchy were long gone on 7 July 1962. A now typically filthy 1018 COUNTY OF LEICESTER with a rag-tag of empties at Iver, a couple of months before withdrawal. Stephen Gradidge.

In fine fettle at Penzance shed, 9 April 1960. The different
arrangement of the extra oil piping casing is more evident in
this view. An additional third piece of casing/piping, visible in
various views, is particularly clear here, low down on the
boiler front and disappearing under the smokebox saddle.
This was present from the beginning, on both sides. R.C. Riley,
transporttreasury.co.uk

1019 COUNTY OF MERIONETH

To traffic 2/4/46

Mileages and Boilers

From new		9919
4/2/49	118,156	C9921
30/8/50	191,327	C9919
25/3/52	257,040	C9913
8/12/53	332,811	C9908
27/7/55	401,680	C9918
3/7/57	479,894	C9926
25/3/59	553,173	C9925
9/1/61	612,371	C9907

Sheds and Works

20/4/46	Newton Abbot
17/5/46	Penzance
10/9/46	Penzance Shops **R**
24/9/46	Newton Abbot Works **L**
13/2/47	Penzance Shops **R**
24/2/47	Newton Abbot Works **L**
29/5/47	Swindon Works **L**
12/1/48	Penzance Shops **R**
16/4/48	Newton Abbot Works **I**
	Tender work only
13/8/48	Newton Abbot Works **I**
	Tender work only **I**
30/10/48	Newton Abbot
4/1/49	Swindon Works **HG**
7/12/49	Newton Abbot works **U**
30/8/50	Swindon Works **HG**
11/9/50	Swindon Works **U**
	Hot box
28/12/50	Penzance then Laira
1/12/51	Shrewsbury
20/12/51	Shrewsbury Shops **U**
25/3/52	Swindon Works **HI**
27/12/52	Stafford Road

31/3/53	Wolverhampton Works **LC**
8/12/53	Swindon Works **HG**
27/2/54	Swindon
27/7/55	Swindon Works **HG**
3/7/57	Swindon Works **HI**
13/11/58	Swindon Shed **U**
25/3/59	Swindon Works **HG**
8/7/59	Caerphilly Works **LC**
24/2/60	Swindon Works **U**
27/3/60	Swindon Shed **U**
27/7/60	Bath Road **U**
28/10/60	Neyland **U**
9/1/61	Swindon Works **HI**
22/5/62	Swindon Works **HC**
6/10/62	Shrewsbury
16/11/62	Oswestry Works **U**

Transferred to LMR book stock 30/12/62

Tenders

From new	2954 renumbered 119
24/9/53	129
14/6/55	114
24/5/57	111

Final recorded mileage 662,550

Withdrawn 11/2/63

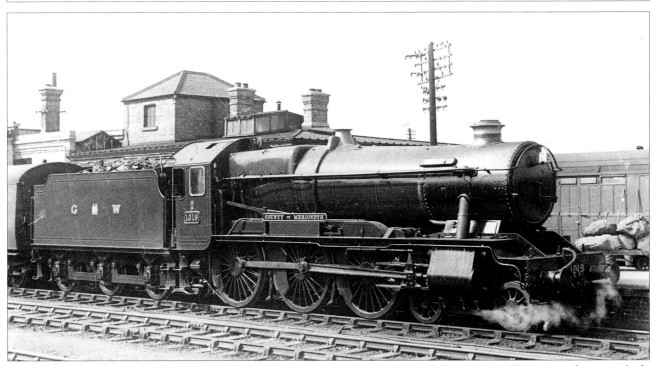

1019 COUNTY OF MERIONETH new (see introductory notes too, page 13) at Swindon on 4 April 1946. Dark green, single chimney; the first to appear already fitted with nameplates. H.C. Casserley, courtesy R.M. Casserley.

1019 COUNTY OF MERIONETH, anonymous in a livery of grey-grime; there are no details with the photograph unfortunately but the 83A Newton Abbot shedplate and BR numberplate indicates the period to be late 1948 to late 1950. The location could well be Long Rock shed, Penzance while the lamp, incidentally, is mounted wrong side to the iron, rendering it out of centre... www.rail-online.co.uk

1019 COUNTY OF MERIONETH gets to grips with the bank at Wellington with a train up from Exeter during 1956. P. Ward.

1020 COUNTY OF MONMOUTH

To traffic 14/12/46

Mileages and Boilers

From new		9920
30/12/48	99,750	C9927
31/8/50	176,994	C9916
20/10/52	260,835	C9926
29/6/54	319,193	C9953
16/5/55	348,990	C9925
13/8/57	430,397	C9925
12/11/58	465,375	C9951
22/11/60	523,357	C9915

Sheds and Works

25/1/47	Laira
17/5/47	Exeter
7/8/47	Bath Road Shops **R**
22/10/47	Newton Abbot works **I**
	Tender Work only
10/9/48	Newton Abbot Works **L**
	Tender Work only
30/10/48	Neyland
30/12/48	Swindon Works **I**
17/5/50	Llanelly Shops **U**
31/8/50	Swindon Works **HG**
7/1/52	Neyland Shops **U**
20/10/52	Swindon Works **HI**
29/6/54	Swindon Works **HC**
16/5/55	Swindon Works **HG**
23/8/56	Swindon Works **LC**
8/9/56	Carmarthen
3/11/56	Neyland
13/8/57	Swindon Works **HI**
12/11/58	Swindon Works **HC**
22/11/60	Swindon Works **HG**
13/9/62	Wolverhampton Works **HC**
3/11/62	St. Philips Marsh
22/3/63	Swindon Works **LC**
2/11/63	Swindon

Tenders

From new		120

Mileage as at 28/12/63 599,291
Withdrawn 26/2/64

1020 COUNTY OF MONMOUTH at Swindon Works, on the same day, more or less, as the view on page 95. 1020 is on one of the turntable stalls, where every GWR 4-6-0 got to stand at least once or twice in its life, it seems. Eric Mountford noted it as one of eight Counties to have received attention at Caerphilly Works, but this does not show on the Record.

Under a year old, 1020 COUNTY OF MONMOUTH at Exeter, briefly its home shed, on 7 September 1947. Green livery, no 'X' under the route availability 'D' disk. R.C. Riley, transporttreasury.co.uk

1020 COUNTY OF MONMOUTH on the turntable at Neyland on 31 July 1951. It had gone to West Wales at the end of 1948. R.C. Riley, transporttreasury.co.uk

1020 COUNTY OF MONMOUTH in the shed yard at Neyand the next day, 1 August 1951, showing off to rather better effect the lined black livery that would have appeared during its 1950 Heavy General. R.C. Riley, transporttreasury.co.uk

At Salisbury, probably on a Portsmouth-Cardiff service.

And glistening in green after its next Heavy General at Swindon, 13 May 1955. R.C. Riley, transporttreasury.co.uk

1021 COUNTY OF MONTGOMERY

To traffic 19/12/46

Mileages and Boilers

From new		9921
12/1/49	96,236	C9924
23/3/50	150,631	C9901
7/6/51	208,492	C9914
23/1/53	298,207	C9953
2/6/54	377,620	C9917
6/1/56	459,885	C9953
20/11/57	535,967	C9953
27/10/59	629,214	C9926
20/3/62	705,661	C9918

Sheds and Works

28/12/46	Old Oak
7/1/48	Reading Shops **R**
24/5/48	Old Oak Shops **L**
11/10/48	Old Oak Shops **R**
12/1/49	Swindon Works **HG**
5/10/49	Old Oak Shops **U**
8/11/49	Chester Shops **U**
23/3/50	Swindon Works **HC**
23/5/50	Old Oak Shops **U**
11/10/50	Old Oak Shops **U**
28/12/50	Laira
7/6/51	Swindon Works **HI**
28/7/52	Laira Shops **U**
9/10/52	Laira Shops **U**
11/12/52	Laira Shops **U**
23/1/53	Swindon Works **HG**
2/6/54	Swindon Works **HI**

4/2/55	Laira Shops **U**
1/3/55	Laira Shops **U**
26/2/55	Penzance
16/7/55	Laira
12/8/55	Laira Shops **U**
8/11/55	Laira Shops **U**
6/1/56	Swindon Works **HG**
21/12/56	Swindon Works **LC**
20/11/57	Swindon Works **HI**
26/3/58	Laira Shops **U**
22/5/58	Laira Shops **U**
7/4/59	Old Oak Shops **U**
8/5/59	Laira Shops **U**
27/10/59	Swindon Works **HG**
28/11/59	Swindon
30/12/59	Swindon Works **cont HG**
31/12/60	St. Philips Marsh
20/3/62	Swindon Works **HI**
4/5/62	Swindon Works **U**
27/7/62	Swindon Works **LC**

Tenders

From new	121
6/1/56	119
20/11/57	127
20/3/62	101

Final recorded mileage 747,718
Withdrawn 1/11/63

1021 leaves Newton Abbot for Plymouth; it was in the West almost for the entirety of the 1950s, only going to Swindon for lesser work at the end of the decade.

1021 COUNTY OF MONTGOMERY, in black, is an up light engine in company with 5918 WALTON HALL on 10 July 1955, heading over Liskeard viaduct. R.C. Riley, transporttreasury.co.uk

Blasting away from Plymouth North Road station, heading for Mutley Tunnel, single chimney 1021 COUNTY OF MONTGOMERY heads an up train in 1956. It was the last to get a double chimney, towards the end of 1959. www.rail-online.co.uk

1021 COUNTY OF MONTGOMERY at Exeter St David's. After its first years at old Oak it had left London for Laira as part of the 1950 re-arranging of the class. Remaining in the West until expelled by dieselisation, it went to those 'elephants graveyards' Swindon then St Philips March, in swift succession. M. Robertson, transporttreasury.co.uk

Late on at Swindon, on 3 June 1962 when a St Philips Marsh engine; extra casing for lubricator pipe. There are two Castles behind, 5035 and 5024, with a King and pannier tank newly traversed out of the main shop, 6002 and 9672. www.rail-online.co.uk

Full grime livery at Shrewsbury shed.

1022 COUNTY OF NORTHAMPTON

To traffic 24/12/46

Mileages and Boilers

From new		9922
17/1/49	88,209	C9920
21/9/50	174,249	C9926
19/8/52	242,145	C9928
14/9/54	307,378	C9928
3/5/56	365,120	C9917
5/5/58	444,433	C9921
21/6/60	516,705	C9953

Sheds and Works

25/1/47	Laira
20/5/47	Penzance Shops **R**
2/7/47	Newton Abbot Works **L**
10/11/47	Newton Abbot Works **L** Tender work only
3/2/48	Penzance Shops **R**
24/5/48	Newton Abbot Works **L** Tender work only
4/9/48	Newton Abbot
30/10/48	Laira
27/11/48	Penzance
17/1/49	Swindon Works **HG**
29/1/49	Laira
27/5/49	Laira Shops **U**
1/2/50	Laira Shops **U**
14/6/50	Laira Shops **U**
21/9/50	Swindon Works **HG**
7/1/51	Laira Shops **U**
1/12/51	Shrewsbury
29/12/51	Chester

4/2/52	Shrewsbury Shops **U**
19/8/52	Swindon Works **HG**
23/2/53	Swindon Works **LC**
15/6/53	Chester Shops **U**
7/8/53	Chseter Shops **U**
24/3/54	Chester Shops **U**
14/9/54	Swindon Works **HI**
23/2/55	Chester Shops **U**
15/7/55	Chester shops **U**
3/5/56	Swindon Works **HG**

Transferred to LMR book stock 23/2/58*

5/5/58	Swindon Books **HI**

Returned to WR book stock 15/6/58

14/6/58	Shrewsbury
25/9/58	Shrewsbury Shops **U**
24/3/59	Stafford Road Shops **U**
8/8/59	Hereford
31/10/59	Shrewsbury
21/6/60	Swindon Works **HG**
26/1/62	Neath Shops **U**
24/3/62	Shrewsbury Shops **U**

*Chester transferred to LMR

Tenders

From new	122
27/6/52	108
22/7/54	122
21/6/60	125

Final recorded mileage 590,659
Withdrawn 5/10/62

The Counties were put to good use in the West on perishables; milk all year round and other valuable comestibles in season. 1022 COUNTY OF NORTHAMPTON in an unlikely alliance with pannier tank 4679 comes off the Royal Albert Bridge on the afternoon of 26 June 1951, with a train of potatoes largely loaded in cattle wagons. A. Lathey, transporttreasury.co.uk

In the Spartan repair bays at Chester shed, 24 June 1956. H.C. Casserley, courtesy R.M. Casserley.

1022 COUNTY OF NORTHAMPTON at rest in the engine yard at Ranelagh Bridge outside Paddington, 18 May 1956. 1022 would not have worked all the way from Chester; that would surely have more than half emptied the tender, requiring a run out to Old Oak. 'SC' plate on smokebox door. R.C. Riley, transporttreasury.co.uk

Newly double chimneyed 1022 COUNTY OF NORTHAMPTON in 1956, climbing the final stretch of Hatton bank, north-west of Warwick, with the 9.18am Margate-Birkenhead. Michael Mensing.

The 9.30am Bournemouth West to Birkenhead train coasting downhill from West Bromwich, Saturday 3 August 1957. Michael Mensing.

1022 COUNTY OF NORTHAMPTON with a Birkenhead-Margate train at Hatton, 23 September 1957. Michael Mensing.

Newly outshopped at Swindon, 3 May 1958. Ron Smith, transporttreasury.co.uk

1023 COUNTY OF OXFORD

To traffic 1/1/47

Mileages and Boilers

From new		9923
22/11/48	81,036	C9925
29/6/50	130,748	C9924
26/6/51	175,572	C9924
15/4/53	254,734	C9912
25/2/55	348,684	C9907
31/5/57	427,367	C9904
10/1/60	514,694	C9929

Sheds and Works

25/1/47	Laira
19/4/47	Truro
17/9/47	Truro Shops **R**
19/9/47	Newton Abbot Works **L**
16/4/48	Newton Abbot Works **L**
28/5/48	Newton Abbot Works **L** Tender work only
21/7/48	Newton Abbot Works **L** Tender work only
22/11/48	Swindon Works **I**
27/11/48	Exeter
4/3/49	Taunton Shops **U**
29/6/50	Swindon Works **HC**
30/12/50	Penzance
9/5/51	Penzance Shops **U**
26/6/51	Swindon Works **HI**
8/9/51	Truro
23/5/52	Swindon Works **LC**

15/4/53	Swindon Works **HG**
25/2/55	Swindon Works **HI**
2/1/56	Swindon Works **LC**
1/3/56	Newton Abbot Works **U**
29/3/56	Newton Abbot Works **U**
21/9/56	Swindon Works **LC**
31/5/57	Swindon Works **HG**
28/6/57	Swindon Works **LC**
20/2/58	Newton Abbot Works **LC**
8/7/58	Swindon Works **HC**
3/10/59	Exeter
10/1/60	Swindon Works **HI**
25/3/61	Swindon
16/2/62	Swindon Works **HC**
6/10/62	Shrewsbury

Transferred to LMR book stock 30/1/62*

*See entry under 1002

Tenders

From new	123
2/4/52	118
12/2/53	119
5/11/55	127
13/3/57	114
14/5/58	110
22/8/61	116

Final recorded mileage 592,957
Withdrawn 1/3/63

GWR livery on 1023 COUNTY OF OXFORD at Truro, 17 June 1947. 1023 went to Truro more or less new in 1947, the largest locomotive to have been stationed there. It became something of the pride of the place and was kept spotless; it was put to work on the shed's principal job, the 8.40pm Penzance-Plymouth, and stayed on that duty for over a year. R.C. Riley, transporttreasury.co.uk

1023 COUNTY OF OXFORD passing Lostwithiel, 11 June 1956. It's not often you see a British steam locomotive at work and a Mediterranean Yacca tree in the same picture. Michael Mensing.

1023 COUNTY OF OXFORD with the 3.35pm Penzance-Truro stopping train, beginning the descent of the 1 in 71/80 to Truro, 16 May 1959. Michael Mensing.

1023 COUNTY OF OXFORD with a down freight on Dainton bank at an unknown date; double chimney was fitted from May 1957 and the second emblem wasn't intoduced until April 1957. P. Ward.

1024 COUNTY OF PEMBROKE

To traffic 9/1/47

Mileages and Boilers

From new		9924
24/12/48	84,139	C9926
21/7/50	150,848	C9900
9/4/52	223,625	C9918
30/6/54	223,625	C9900
14/6/56	381,542	C9901
10/7/58	445,105	C9910
2/3/60	534,725	C9954
15/12/61	596,547	C9901

Sheds and Works

2/1/47	Stafford Road
11/12/47	Stafford Road Shops **R**
17/8/48	Banbury Shops **R**
19/10/48	Taunton Shops **R**
24/12/48	Swindon Works **I**
27/4/50	Stafford Road Shops **U**
21/7/50	Swindon Works **HG**
4/11/50	Shrewsbury Shops
24/2/51	Laira
13/7/51	Laira Shops **U**
17/8/51	Laira Shops **U**
5/12/51	Newton Abbot Works **U**
9/4/52	Swindon Works **HI**
17/9/52	Laira Shops **U**
4/10/52	Old Oak
1/11/52	Chester
18/2/53	Tyseley Shops **LC**
7/8/53	Tyseley Shops **LC**
28/3/54	Chester Shops **U**
30/6/54	Swindon Works **HG**
3/3/55	Stafford Road Shops **U**

20/8/55	Chester Shops **U**
9/12/55	Chester shops **U**
14/6/56	Swindon Works **HI**
29/5/57	Chester Shops **U**
10/1/58	Stafford Road Shops **U**

Transferred to LMR book stock 23/2/58*

14/6/58	Bath Road
10/7/58	Swindon Works **HG**

Returned to WR book stock 15/6/58

2/3/60	Swindon Works **HI**
25/5/60	Reading Shops **U**
10/9/60	St. Philips Marsh
26/4/61	St. Philips Marsh **U**
15/12/61	Swindon Works **HG**
10/7/62	Hereford Shops **U**
7/2/63	Wolverhampton Works **HC**
29/3/63	Wolverhampton Works **contHC**
22/7/63	Stourbridge Shops **U**
2/11/63	Swindon
20/1/64	Wolverhampton Works **U**

*Chester transferred to LMR

Tenders

From new	124
29/5/54	126
12/7/58	108
2/3/59	106
15/12/61	127

Mileage to 28/12/63 643,975
Withdrawn 8/4/64

1024 COUNTY OF PEMBROKE comes through Gwinear Road on 29 August 1958. Double chimney, second tender emblem; good view of both plug covers on top of boiler ahead of safety valve bonnet. L.W. Rowe, Colour-Rail.

Ex-works at Swindon, parked next to a non-County tender to present an odd picture. Different style of casing bridging boiler and smokebox. transporttreasury.co.uk

1024 COUNTY OF PEMBROKE far from its Chester home at Teignmouth in 1957. This was one of the eight noted by Eric Mountford as receiving attention at Caerphilly Works, but the visit went unrecorded. transporttreasury.co.uk

Fine low light at Canton; 5967 BICKMARSH HALL beyond and another County in the early 1960s. All the locos have the detested 'cobbles' in the tenders. George Heiron, courtesy Mrs Shirley Heiron, transporttreasury.co.uk

1025 COUNTY OF RADNOR

To traffic 20/1/47

Mileages and Boilers

From new		9925
14/10/48	75,7575	C9918
13/9/49	109,328	C9929
17/10/50	160,827	C9929
4/11/50	161,657	[in store]
2/5/52	218,120	C9919
23/2/54	292,382	C9901
6/5/56	365,743	C9922
10/1/57	434,302	C9922
26/8/59	486,798	C9905
21/2/61	535,343	C9913

Shops and Works

22/2/47	Stafford Road
3/5/48	Stafford Road Shops **L**
14/10/48	Swindon Works **I**
13/9/49	Swindon Works **HC**
17/10/50	Swindon Works **HI**
4/11/50	Shrewsbury
1/10/51	Tyseley Shops **U**
9/1/52	Shrewsbury Shops **U**
2/5/52	Swindon Works **HI**
31/12/52	Shrewsbury Shops **U**
15/4/53	Shrewsbury Shops **U**
23/2/54	Swindon Works **HG**
11/12/54	Shrewsbury Shops **U**
21/4/55	Laira Shops **U**
21/6/55	Laira Shops **U**
6/4/56	Swindon Works **HG**
10/1/57	Swindon Works **HI**
16/12/58	Wolverhampton Works **HC**
26/8/59	Swindon Works **HC**
5/10/59	Old Oak **U**
10/2/60	Shrewsbury Shops **U**
21/2/61	Swindon Works **HI**
25/5/62	Shrewsbury Shops **U**
30/10/62	Oswestry Works **U**

Transferred to LMR book stock 30/12/62

Tenders

From new	125
25/10/50	102
28/3/52	123
1/3/56	102
26/1/60	117

Final recorded mileage 601,069
Withdrawn 18/2/63

1025 COUNTY OF RADNOR with a Bournemouth-Wolverhampton Low Level (and probably beyond) train approaching Olton on Saturday 10 August 1957, the end of the Birmingham Holiday Weeks. Michael Mensing.

Shrewsbury's grimy black liveried 1025 COUNTY OF RADNOR, at Oxford on 8 May 1954. Norman Preedy Archive.

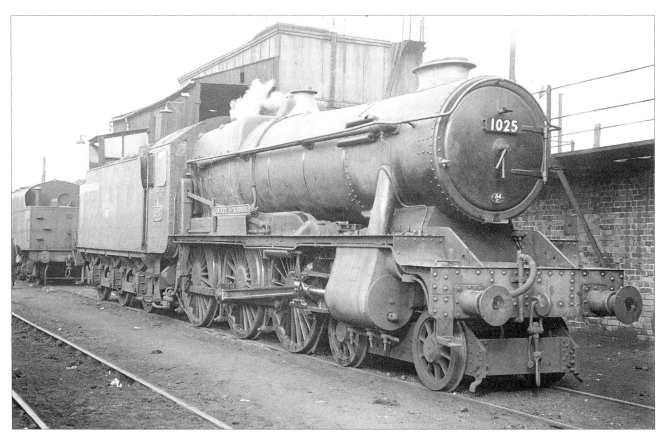

1025 COUNTY OF RADNOR alongside the coal stage at Shrewsbury, 14 February 1960. Final arrangement of casing on smokebox. Towards the end, Shrewsbury became a sort of last redoubt for active Counties. Alec Swain, transporttreasury.co.uk

Once it went to Shrewsbury from Stafford Road in 1950 1025 stayed there, even transferring officially to LMR 'book stock' when Shrewsbury passed to the London Midland, though for operating and maintenance purposes it was more or less irrelevant. This is Chester shed in the 1960s; the shed itself is over there in the murk, hidden by the bulk of the loco and the turntable (behind that second, distant, loco) was entirely separate, inside a triangle of running lines and, you suspect, an operating annoyance at the least. www.rail-online.co.uk

At Chester looking good in BR dark green; it was one of the last to get a double chimney, at a Heavy Casual in August 1959 and doubtless it has just arrived back from Swindon from that work. It probably got the modified superheating and piping/casing at the same time. It will probably never look this good again. www.rail-online.co.uk

1025 at Chester. transporttreasury.co.uk

1026 COUNTY OF SALOP

To traffic 31/1/47

Mileages and Boilers

From new		9926
29/10/48	86,599	C9916
21/2/50	150,933	C9902
24/1/51	194,007	C9902
13/8/52	270,190	C9929
18/12/53	338,752	C9929
20/6/55	388,970	C9911
13/8/56	433,879	C9900
3/10/58	494,474	C9950
16/9/60	554,436	C9906

Sheds and Works

22/3/47	Old Oak
2/7/47	Old Oak Shed **R**
16/11/47	Old Oak Shed **R**
10/3/48	Old Oak Shops **R**
29/10/48	Swindon Works **I**
9/2/49	Old Oak Shops **U**
16/6/49	Old Oak Shops **U**
21/2/50	Swindon Works **HC**
1/8/50	Old Oak Shops **U**
24/1/51	Swindon Works **HI**
13/8/52	Swindon Works **HG**
4/10/52	Laira
21/2/53	Bath Road
18/12/53	Swindon Works **HI**
27/3/54	Chester
20/6/55	Swindon Works **HG**
5/11/55	Shrewsbury
13/8/56	Swindon Works **HI**
11/6/57	Shrewsbury Shops **U**
22/10/57	Wolverhampton Works **U**
3/10/58	Swindon Works **HC**
10/9/59	Shrewsbury Shops **U**
23/10/59	Shrewsbury shops **U**
7/5/60	Shrewsbury Shops **U**
16/9/60	Swindon Works **HI**

Tenders

From new	126
21/6/52	122
22/7/54	108
3/10/59	126

Apparently 'at one point' 1026 had narrow Hawksworth tender 4070, originally built for Modified Hall 6991

Final recorded mileage 621,007
Withdrawn 13/9/62

1026 COUNTY OF SALOP at The Hawthorns football ground halt, Handsworth Junction, Birmingham, 1961. Michael Mensing.

1026 COUNTY OF SALOP at Swindon after overhauls; first in February 1950 in black after a Heavy Casual and secondly in green, acquired during a Heavy Intermediate in August 1956. R.C. Riley and R. Wilson, transporttreasury.co.uk

1026 COUNTY OF SALOP, entering Shrewsbury station with a train from Chester; still single chimney, 22 June 1957. B.W.L Brooksbank, Initial Photographics.

Shrewsbury again, with 1026, now of course with double chimney, about 1960. Colour-Rail.

1026 at Leamington Spa. transporttreasury.co.uk

1027 COUNTY OF STAFFORD

To traffic 11/3/47

Mileage and Boilers

From new		9927
16/12/48	77,265	C9923
6/10/50	166,592	C9927
23/12/52	260,014	C9925
24/1/55	345,327	C9927
31/8/56	404,649	C9921
15/4/58	467,723	C9906
13/6/60	538,770	C9910
12/4/62	600,212	C9912

Sheds and Works

22/3/47	Westbury
20/12/47	Westbury Shops **R**
25/5/48	Bath Road Shops **L**
1/9/48	Reading Shops **R**
16/12/48	Swindon Works **I**
21/1/49	Laira Shops **U**
30/6/49	Weymouth Shops **U**
14/4/50	Bath Road Shops **U**
6/10/50	Swindon Works **HG**
4/11/50	Neyland
12/9/52	Swindon Works **U**
12/9/52	Llanelly **U**
23/12/52	Swindon Works **HI**
24/1/55	Swindon Works **HI**
18/4/56	Ebbw Jct. Shops **U**
31/8/56	Swindon Works **HG**
27/1/58	Neyland Shops **U**
15/4/458	Swindon Works **HG**

29/10/59	Danygraig Shops **U**
28/11/59	Bath Road
13/6/60	Swindon Works **HI**
10/9/60	St. Philips Marsh
6/2/61	St. Philips Marsh Shops **U**
2/5/61	Barrow Road Shops **U**
18/8/61	Barrow Road Shops **U**
7/10/61	Neyland
16/10/61	Neyland Shops **U**
12/4/62	Swindon Works **HG**

Transferred to LMR book stock 24/2/63*

23/3/63	Shrewsbury
28/5/63	Shrewsbury Shops **U**

Transferred to WR book stock 8/9/63

29/9/63	Swindon

*See entry under 1002

Tenders

From new	127
18/11/52	100
29/11/54	112
15/4/58	125
18/6/60	122
12/4/62	104

Final recorded mileage 650,666
Withdrawn 25/10/63

1027 COUNTY OF STAFFORD with block number to bufferbeam, running into Paddington on 24 July 1947. The loco is a lovely dark green under the all-conquering grime grey, which seemed to largely reign in the straitened late 1940s. Colour-Rail.

Black-liveried 1027 COUNTY OF STAFFORD at Cardiff General, 14 March 1953. Stephen Gradidge.

Shining amongst the other, grimier, denizens at Neyland after an overhaul – the year is not given though its double chimney fitted in August 1956 suggest it might be later that year. It was at this Pembrokeshire outpost for almost the entirety of the 1950s. J. Leaf, Colour-Rail.

Passing Iver on 1 July 1961, curiously without a shedplate. Stephen Gradidge.

1028 COUNTY OF WARWICK

To traffic 26/3/47

Mileages and Boilers

From new		9928
4/3/49	102,165	C9919
9/5/50	166,388	C9915
14/5/51	209,661	C9915
18/2/53	288,548	C9915
20/10/54	368,182	C9906
16/3/56	436,152	C9924
12/8/58	529,477	C9908
30/3/60	602,944	C9914
20/3/62	668,329	C9916

Sheds and Works

17/5/47	Bath Road
23/12/47	Old Oak Shed **R**
25/11/48	Bath Road Shops **L**
	Tender work only
4/3/49	Swindon Works **HG**
9/5/50	Swindon Works **HC**
14/5/51	Swindon Works **HI**
18/2/53	Swindon Works **HI**
16/7/53	Hereford Shops **U**
20/1/054	Swindon Works **HG**
16/3/56	Swindon Works **HI**
12/6/56	Swindon Works **LC**
13/3/57	Swindon Works **HC**
12/8/58	Swindon Works **HG**
18/9/59	Bath Road Shops **U**
13/10/59	Shrewsbury Shops **U**
5/11/59	Bath Road Shops **U**
30/3/60	Swindon Works **HI**
10/9/60	St. Philips Marsh
2/8/61	Oswestry Works **LC**
20/3/62	Swindon Works **HG**
15/1/63	Gloucester Shops **U**
14/6/63	Swansea East Dock Shops **U**
2/11/63	Swindon

Tenders

From new	128
12/6/56	107
12/3/57	106
12/8/58	112
20/3/62	113

Final recorded mileage 723,639
Withdrawn 2/12/63

1028 COUNTY OF WARWICK leaving Parson's Tunnel with a down express, teatime 11 August 1951. A. Lathey, transporttreasury.co.uk

1028 COUNTY OF WARWICK leaving Par on 9 July 1955. The projection on the firebox shoulder is not some odd form of washout plug but the little bell-shaped cup/cover, hanging upside down by one of its two bolts. R.C. Riley, transporttreasury.co.uk

1028 COUNTY OF WARWICK at Exeter St David's, August 1955; a washout plug cover flapping in the wind again... A. Lathey, transporttreasury.co.uk

1029 COUNTY OF WORCESTER

To traffic 10/4/47

Mileages and Boilers

From new		9929
30/6/49	93,826	C9917
5/4/51	166,666	C9950
9/1/53	245,294	C9950
2/4/54	290,982	C9912
1/3/55	321,522	C9916
8/1/57	392,997	C9916
11/2/58	424,495	C9915
11/5/59	457,909	C9917
23/6/60	492,351	C9909

Sheds and Works

19/4/47	Stafford Road
31/12/47	Stafford Road Shed **R**
20/7/48	Hereford Shops **R**
8/11/48	Wolverhampton Works **L**
30/6/49	Swindon Works **HG**
11/9/50	Stafford Road Shed **LC**
28/10/50	Wolverhampton Works **U**
5/4/51	Swindon Works **HG**
9/4/52	Stafford Road Shed **U**
23/10/52	Old Oak Shops **U**
9/1/53	Wolverhampton Works **HI**
26/12/53	Neyland
2/4/54	Swindon Works **HC**
1/1/55	Neyland Shops **U**
1/3/55	Swindon Works **HG**
8/1/57	Swindon Works **HI**
11/2/58	Swindon Works **HC**
28/3/59	To store at Llanelly
11/5/59	Swindon Works **HC**
23/6/60	Swindon Works **HI**
30/6/61	Swindon Works **HC**
12/8/61	Swindon

Tenders

From new	129
27/9/53	104
11/5/59	105

Final recorded mileage 555,216
Withdrawn 5/12/62

1029 COUNTY OF WORCESTER, ex-works at Swindon shed in May 1951. This too was one of the eight Counties that Eric Mountford observed undergoing attention at Caerphilly Works, but again it does not show in the Record.

At Cardiff still in black, 30 August 1956. Its previous Heavy General had ended a couple of months before BR dark green began to be applied, in May 1955, so it was amongst the last, or the last, to emerge from Swindon still in black. Stephen Gradidge.

End of a County. Withdrawn at the end of 1962, 1029 lingered on at Swindon, like many other engines. It was thus frequently photographed, though often the photographers seemed unclear as to its identity. It is uplifting, observing this intact but doomed County, to reflect that a new one is rapidly taking shape at the Great Western Society's Didcot shed, works and display ground. Stephen Gradidge.

Endpiece

John Robertson, transporttreasury.co.uk